NOTES

ON THE

LAND TENURES AND REVENUE ASSESSMENTS

OF

UPPER INDIA

NOTES
ON THE
LAND TENURES AND REVENUE ASSESSMENTS
OF
UPPER INDIA

PATRICK CARNEGY

GYAN

Published by

GYAN

Gyan Publishing House
5, Ansari Road
Daryaganj, New Delhi-110002
Phone: 011-47034999, 9811692060
E-mail: books@gyanbooks.com

Distribution Network
gyanbooks.com
India, USA, Canada, UK, Australia

ISBN: 978-93-7133-026-8 (PB)

First Published, 1874

2nd Impression 2025

Printed at: Gyan Press, Delhi.

NOTES ON THE LAND TENURES AND REVENUE ASSESSMENTS OF UPPER INDIA
Author: PATRICK CARNEGY

NOTES

ON THE

LAND TENURES AND REVENUE ASSESSMENTS

OF

UPPER INDIA.

BY

PATRICK CARNEGY,

OF H.M.'S INDIAN SERVICE, AND COMMISSIONER IN OUDH.

LONDON:

TRÜBNER & CO., 57 & 59 LUDGATE HILL.

1874.

CONTENTS.

INTRODUCTORY REMARKS.

On the 6th of Oct. 1858, Lord Canning, the first Viceroy of India, reiterating the words of Sir Robert Montgomery, the then Chief Commissioner of Oudh, wrote the following memorable sentences.

"Recent events have very much shaken the Governor-General's faith in the stability of the village system, even in our older provinces, and his lordship is, therefore, all the more disposed to abandon it, in a province to which it was unknown before our rule was introduced in 1856. The Governor-General is well aware, that in some of the districts of the North-western Provinces, the holders of villages belonging to tallukdārs, which had been broken up at the Settlement, acknowledged the suzerainty of the tallukdārs as soon as our authority was subverted. They acted, in fact, as though they regarded the arrangement made at the Settlement as valid, and to be maintained just as long as British rule lasted, and no longer, and as though they wished the tallukdār to re-assert his former rights, and resume his ancient position over them at the first opportunity. Their conduct amounts almost to an admission, that their own rights, whatever these may be, are subordinate to those of the tallukdārs;

that they do not value the recognition of these rights by the ruling authority; and that the tallukdāri system is the ancient, indigenous, and cherished system of the country. If such be the case in our older provinces, where our system of Government has been established for more than half a century, during twenty years of which we have done our best to uphold the interest of the village occupant against the interest and influence of the tallukdār, much more will the same feeling prevail in the province of Oudh, where village occupancy, independent and free from subordination to the tallukdārs, has been unknown. Our endeavour to better, as we thought, the village occupants in Oudh, has not been appreciated by them. It may be true that these men had not influence and weight enough to aid us in restoring order, but they had *numbers*, and it can hardly be doubted that, if they had valued their restored rights, they would have shown some signs of a willingness to support the Government which revived these rights. But they have done nothing of the kind. The Governor-General is, therefore, of opinion that these village occupants, as such, deserve little consideration from us.

"On these grounds, as well as because the tallukdārs, if they will, can materially assist in the re-establishment of our authority and the restoration of tranquillity, the Governor-General has determined that a Tallukdāri Settlement shall be made. His lordship desires that it may be so framed as to secure the village occupants from extortion; that the tallukdārs should, on no account, be invested with any police authority; that the tenures should be declared to be contingent on a certain specified service to be rendered; and that the assessment should be so moderate as to leave an ample margin for all expenses incidental to the performance of such service. The tallukdārs may then be legitimately expected to aid the authorities of Government by their personal influence, and their own active co-operation; and they may be required, under penalties, to undertake all the duties and responsibilities, which by the regulations of the Government properly pertain to land-holders. These duties should be rigidly exacted and enforced."

It has been alike the duty and privilege of the writer, as Settlement Officer and Commissioner, to devote ten years of his life to carrying into effect the Settlement of Oudh, based on the above instructions of H. M.'s first Viceroy. There are few subjects that are more involved and difficult than the land tenures of Upper India, and although their elucidation has taxed the intelligence of the most brilliant men in the Indian services, we have still much to learn before our information on the subject can be considered complete. The officers of the Oudh Settlement Department had unusual opportunities of arriving at a correct estimate of tenures, owing to the circumstance that in Oudh alone has the plan, since then much discussed, been followed, of intrusting the judicial determination of all rights in the soil, at the time of making the first revised land Settlement, to the officers of that Department.

The writer's duties have lain in that portion of the province in which, perhaps, the different forms of land tenure are more varied and complicated than elsewhere; much attention has therefore been paid to this branch of the subject, and many decisions, reports, and memoranda have necessarily been the result. He imagines that some of his papers, recording the opinions formed on data most laboriously collected, may be found of use, if not to the general reader, at least to those who may come after him in the Indian Government service. He has, therefore, devoted a portion of his furlough leisure to editing such of them as were within his reach in England, and these form the subject of the present volume.

P. CARNEGY.

HAZELWOOD, UPPER NORWOOD,
April 1874.

LAND TENURES AND REVENUE ASSESSMENTS

OF

UPPER INDIA.

CHAPTER I.

ON LAND TENURES GENERALLY, AS JUDICIALLY DETERMINED BY THE FAIZABAD SETTLEMENT COURTS; (AN OFFICIAL REPORT.)

THE judicial work of the Faizabad Settlement has, in accordance with instructions, been taken up according to Parganas, and proprietary and subproprietary rights have been disposed of as follows:—All proprietary rights in independent estates, and all subproprietary claims to whole villages or specific portions of villages have already been disposed of, and claims to shares or to specific lands, groves, &c., remain for determination. When the field-survey had prepared the way, and we were in a position to commence inquiries into rights, the prescribed thirty-days' notice to advance claims was duly issued in each village.

In tallukdāri villages it was generally found that there was but a single claim to sub-settlement; but in independent villages the claims to proprietary title were numerous, and continued to be given in until the second or fifteen-days' notice, under Ruling No. 16, was issued, which was when the case-work was well advanced. As soon as this was perceived, our efforts were first directed to the disposal of the former class of cases, and many of the latter class were allowed to lie over till towards the end.

In those independent villages in which, notwithstanding the issue of the two notices, no claim to the proprietary title was advanced, the initiative was taken by this Department; the present holder was summoned, his title examined, and, where found complete, his proprietary position was decreed.

All claims to a village were, in the first instance, taken up together, and formed a single record of inquiry; but a good deal of confusion followed this course, owing to the impossibility of bringing all the parties and their evidence together in regular order. To get rid of this confusion, we for a time took up each claim, and disposed of it separately; but this caused additional labour. We finally adopted the present procedure, which is our first plan improved upon. All claims of the same nature in a village are taken up at the same time; each has a distinct number, and is carefully indexed on the fly-leaf; all the proofs are kept apart, according to cases; one Kānūngo's report, one reply by the defendant, and one judgment, does for the whole village, and each has its separate decree. When the same pleadings and particulars apply to several villages, the record of inquiry is made with reference to the principal or parent village, and a note is filed with the papers of all the other villages referring to it for details. It may be here noted that claims to share are being taken up according to estates (*mahals*), and not according to villages (*mauzas*).

Titles to land are divided into two great classes, proprietary and subproprietary. In the pre-historic period the country was possessed by Bhars, the oldest known inhabitants, and the manner in which these people were eventually replaced by certain clans and families, who still have their representatives, has already been detailed in various historical reports.

First, All present proprietary titles have been acquired since the overthrow of the Bhars within the last five hundred years, by (1) usurpation, (2) purchase, (3) grant or charter, (4) reclamation of waste, or (5), by gift. A sixth method has been suggested, viz., by *inheritance,* where the origin of the tenure has been lost in obscurity; but as the property must at the outset have been *acquired* by one of the above five means, before it could be transmitted to heirs, it is preferable to leave that method out of the list.

Second, All existing subproprietary titles may be traced to (1) former proprietorship, (2) purchase, and (3) relationship, and are commonly known by the vernacular terms marginally indicated. Of these, Nos. 1 to 7 carry with them a heritable and transferable title; No. 8 is subject to special conditions; and No. 9 is altogether contingent. It must be understood that there are different grades of subproprietors. There are, in fact, subproprietors *within* subproprietors, the titles of the *minor* class having been obtained in any of the three ways just indicated, by which the *major* class came by their rights. Rights have now been detailed; we shall next proceed to define them.

1. Pukhtadīri.
2. Dīdāri.
3. Sīr.
4. Nankār.
5. Shankalap.
6. Birt.
7. Bai-kitāt.
8. Baghāt; and,
9. Biswi.

Proprietary title.—The superior right in tallukas, however or whenever acquired, has been declared by the British Government to have been for ever conferred, and the Sanad under which it is held represents the title-deed or charter.

Claims to the superior proprietary title in villages which are in tallukas have therefore been at once summarily dismissed. The only exception there could be to the above rule would be in villages mortgaged to the tallukdār within limitations, to the redemption of which the Sanad is no longer to be urged as a bar; but no cases of this nature have as yet been brought forward. For further details of the tallukdāri tenure, reference is invited to the historical essay on that subject further on. In independent villages, proprietary titles have come under inquiry, and the cases have been disposed of on their merits. In this class are included claims advanced by tallukdārs for villages which were not entered in their Sanads, owing to their not having been in their estates when the Province came under our rule, and in which the tallukdār had to come into court like any other suitor.

Claims were disposed of on the following principles :—(1) Those which were barred by the law of limitations were summarily dismissed. (2) If the property claimed was included in the defendant's estate, within limitations, but without any legal transfer of proprietary rights, the claim was decreed. (3) Where it happened that the incorporation took place beyond the term of limitations, and without a valid transfer of rights, the procedure at different times adopted has been somewhat conflicting. It was at first ruled that subproprietors could not be recognised in independent estates, as the full proprietary title must be decreed to the one party or the other, as the case might be. Subsequently it was held, that if the party under engagement with Government had received from the party in possession an appreciable beneficiary interest for a period beyond limitation, it should be continued to him. A good deal of correspondence ensued on the subject of the above conflicting rulings, which eventuated in the latter of the two principles being maintained; but it remains to be decided whether the party out of possession is, under such circumstances, to be admitted to engage for the Revenue.

A third of the villages of the area under review are broken up and distributed over different Mahals, or estates; the other two-thirds are held as whole villages by the proprietors. This heart-rending intermixed tenure was created as follows:—As the offspring of the common ancestor increased and multiplied, divisions of ancestral property gradually took place, and these were effected by each member taking one or more entire villages, and portions of other villages, the area of land and proportion of rental constituting each ancestral share being adjusted with reference to the area and rental of the entire estate. And this was followed by each party thenceforward engaging direct with the native government for his now distinct estate. In the villages of which portions only had to be assigned to different members, the subdivision of arable land was generally made in blocks (*chakbat*), and not by fields (*khetbat*). There were two ways of dividing the waste-land, including the habitations. In some estates it is all held in common, and in others it was partly subdivided and partly held in common.

When by the process just described one estate had expanded into several separate properties, it not infrequently happened afterwards that one or more of these properties was overtaken by misfortune, and the proprietors were reduced to every sort of shift to save their land, or to make the most they could in parting with it. One member of the community would seek the protection of a chief of his own clan, and make over his holding in trust to him; another would take his holding to that chief's rival, in view of establishing a balance of power, lest the whole village should be absorbed by the first chief; a third would court the official protection of the Kānūngo; a fourth would crave shelter from a Brahman of note, relying on his sacred calling to secure his possession; a fifth would mortgage to a money-lender; and a sixth might sell to a neighbouring capitalist; and the result of all this would be that people of different tribes and persuasions, varying in number from two to ten, would gain, and did gain, a footing in these subdivided villages. A great difficulty had to be encountered in the fact that the record of these holdings, as found in the public offices, did not by any means tally with actual possession, for which the following reasons are assigned :—(1) After subdivision, some of the coparceners reclaimed more of the waste-land held in common than others. (2) The co-sharer A lived in village Z, and the co-sharer B in village Y. It suited A best to have his cultivation near his house, and he therefore took up B's share in addition to his own in village Z. The same applied to B in regard to the lands of A in Y. Such exchanges were often made under agreement, and sometimes by compulsion; and although the possession of parties through these means often varied, the ancestral holdings remained recorded, till annexation, as they were originally entered in the Pargana Registers. The reason for this is easily assigned. No pains were ever taken, in the king's time, to ascertain the individual responsibilities of the different members of the brotherhood; and the assessments were always made by fixing a lump sum at random on an estate, and not with reference to the capabilities of the individual villages of which it was composed.

Every effort has been made during revision of settlement

to correct the record of fractional holdings. Three points had to be kept in view, and, if possible, reconciled—(1) *ancestral* share, (2) *recorded* share, and (3) *possessed* share. Our inquiries soon led to the conclusion that the proprietary communities, as a rule, were desirous that the holdings to be recorded at this settlement should be shown in accordance with long-existing possession, rather than according to ancestral share. They were encouraged to carry this out to the utmost extent amongst themselves, without resort to Government officials. This has resulted in this trying portion of the work being disposed of in a satisfactory manner, without extraneous intervention, and with comparatively little trouble to this Department. The people have adjusted their respective holdings amongst themselves according to long-existing possession, and an agreement signed by those concerned has been given in, verified, and filed in every village which has holdings in two or more distinct estates.

Allusion was made to our mode of procedure in such cases in the *Annual Report* of 1863-4, which led to the comment that cases were erroneously being taken up about fractional shares, village by village, instead of taking up claims to shares in an entire estate at once. But it had escaped observation that these were not cases relating to shares in a single estate at all. They were claims to proprietary or subproprietary rights in specific portions of a village, the lands of which were found to be, not in a single estate, when the question would naturally have been one of shares, but in from two to ten *different* estates; and therefore the only procedure that could have been carried out was the one adopted and explained above. The fact is, the form of tenure which prevails in Faizabad and Azimgarh is beyond measure perplexing, and it is not generally understood. It is detailed in the "Azimgarh Report," in the Board's printed *Circular*, No. 1, and in the *Oudh Circular*, No. 7, of 1865. A good deal of new light has also been thrown upon it by our reports of the 13th and 16th January 1865. The settlement work of a district is indefinitely prolonged by the existence of this tenure; for, as a matter of fact, every specific holding of the kind in question gives rise to just the same amount of labour that a whole village does elsewhere. These estates are variously composed of villages or portions of villages, and may be classified as follows:—(1) Of one or more entire villages; (2) of one or more entire villages, and one or more specific portions of villages; (3) of portions only of several villages; and (4), of a portion of a single village only, the owner engaging direct with Government, the rest of the village being in other properties. Estates of the last description are known by the name of the village, part of which only they contain. The other three kinds are known by the name of any one of their component villages.

It sometimes occurs that a village, being divided between several estates, gives its name to each of these properties, as for instance Barwārīpūr. The engagement for that village was held by A, when he died, leaving three sons, B, C, and D; they divided their property, each taking a third of Barwārīpūr proper, the parent village, and a portion each of the rest of the family property. They then entered into direct Revenue engagements with the State for their different properties, which were thereafter known as Barwārīpūr B, C, and D respectively. Supposing B to die, and E to succeed, his property would then change its name to Barwārīpūr E, and a similar mutation would take place on every occasion of fresh succession. This is a clumsy way of naming estates, and it is open to objection—firstly, because the name is subject to frequent changes; and, secondly, because it might any day happen that each of the representative proprietors of the three different estates had the same name, in which case we should suffer confusion by having three estates all called, say, Barwārīpūr-Ganga-Sing. To obviate this possibility, it has been arranged, in concert with many of those concerned, that in future the estates shall be known as Barwārīpūr first, second, or third, in the order of family seniority, and the arrangement recommends itself as both simple and permanent.

Class (1) of the four descriptions of estates above indicated is to be found throughout Upper India, but the other three classes are much more rarely met with. The last of these classes has now ceased to exist in the Faizabad District, under an administrative arrangement, by which, in order to obviate a multiplicity of insignificant properties, the owners of such remnants of land have been recommended to attach them to some other neighbouring estate, which they might select. The three other classes remain as before.

One of the moot points of this settlement is, whether an engagement shall be taken for each estate, or for each village. This office memorandum of the 8th July last discussed that question in detail, and set forth the reasons why, in opposition to the practice followed elsewhere, the former, and not the latter course, should be followed. As our views were generally approved by superior authority, they have been carried out, engagements being taken for each estate, and not each village. At the outset of the settlement it was thought that it would be of great advantage if the more influential landholders could be induced to arrange exchanges amongst themselves of their outlying and isolated holdings, so as to reduce their possessions as much as possible to entire villages. Such a measure is strongly advocated in Mr Thomason's "Despatches." The saving of trouble to public officials, and expense to proprietors, if it could have been carried out, would have been incalculable. But experience has proved the impossibility of reconciling so many conflicting interests to the introduction of the reform, and those concerned find ready excuses in the difficulty that undoubtedly exists in finding holdings in which title, area, and profits are so evenly balanced as to induce an exchange. The measure has therefore been reluctantly abandoned.

The rule has been laid down in Oudh of usually appointing a representative of the village community as *Lambardār* for every 500 Rs. of Revenue payable to Government. Where the estate consists of a single village, the letter of this instruction has been obeyed; but where a village is broken up, and its various component holdings are distributed over two or more different estates, in the manner already explained, the instruction could not be precisely followed. For instance, the Government demand from village A is 500 Rs. This village is distributed over the four estates B, C, D, and E, each of which holds a fourth of the area. Each of these separate properties is of course entitled to one representative at least, and so the village is represented by not less than four instead of only one man. There is no remedy for this, short of setting aside the *Mahalwār* principle of settlement altogether. The plan followed in such cases has therefore been to give to every estate in which there are such holdings a representative for each sum of 500 Rs. demandable from it. The object of the rule was to make one of the community responsible for a certain portion of the demand, and to allow a certain remuneration in lieu of this responsibility. These objects are equally gained whether the representative be appointed *Mauzawār*, or *Mahalwār*.

In concluding the portion of this paper devoted to proprietary title, it may be well to mention that the consideration of the subject of distribution of shares and payments of village communities, is reserved for a future address.

Subproprietary title.—It is now proposed to give some account of the subordinate tenures which have been already detailed.

(1.) A *pukhtadāri*, or sub-settled tenures, may be based on (1) former proprietorship, with fairly continuous possession up to annexation,* when the village was incorporated without a valid transfer of rights; (2) purchase of a subordinate tenure, as *Birt*, *Shankalap*, &c., no mutation in the names of proprietors having taken place, and the subproprietor having retained entire control of the village; and (3) the failure of the proprietor to redeem old mortgages, the power to do so having now expired under local rules. In the king's time the holder of any intermediate tenure between the superior and the cultivator was said to hold *pakkā*; and since our rule the name that has firmly attached itself to this description of tenure is *pukhtadāri*, a name that was unknown during native rule.

(2.) *Dīdārī.*—When property was transferred voluntarily or involuntarily, it was by no means an uncommon, though not an invariable rule, for the purchaser to assign a portion of the property in perpetuity to the seller, for his subsistence,

* Changes of procedure were introduced by the Sub-settlement Act of 1866.

under the designation of *Dīdārī*. This might be done (1) by assigning a share equal to a fourth, a sixth, a seventh, an eighth, or a tenth of the property transferred, and land to that extent was then made over, which might be one or more entire villages, or only a few fields; or (2), by giving a certain amount of land at pleasure, without any reference to a specific share. These *Dīdārī* tenures were generally conferred under writing, seldom verbally. When a whole village is held under this tenure, the subproprietor invariably also enjoys all village privileges and dues, and with these the *proprietor* has no concern whatever. The same is also the case where the subproprietor holds an entire and separate fractional portion of a village included in a single estate; but where there are two fractional portions of any village in an estate, one of which is held as *Dīdārī*, and the other is not, it will generally be found that in that case the sub-tenure carries with it no village privileges or dues whatever. In the course of the judicial proceedings, where the tenure was found to extend to the entire village, or entire fractional portion, the sub-settlement was of course decreed; where smaller holdings were being contested, the decree has been based on extracts of the field Registers filed with the proceedings. It may be mentioned that at the outset *Dīdārī* grants were always rent-free, and the majority of these are still so. In some cases, however, a low quit-rent was subsequently assessed, known by the name of *Barbasti*. This item is always found to be considerably below the Government demand. In this class of sub-tenures, which were given in lieu of other superior rights long since absorbed, whether they be held rent-free or at low rates, the superior holder has, of course, to make good the Government demand from his other property. Where the rent-free tenure extends to certain fields only, the other village lands can be held responsible for the Revenue that should properly fall on the rent-free portion, whether the estate in which the village is situated be at some future period broken up or not. But where the rent-free tenure extends to a whole village, or fractional portion of a village, this will not be the case; and it was therefore authoritatively ruled that a condition should be entered in the administration paper, that if the Sadr Malguzār should hereafter fail in his Revenue engagements, these must be taken up by the *Dīdārī* holder; and this rule is being carried out.

(3.) *Sīr.*—Subproprietory *sīr* is of two kinds. *First*, when old proprietors parted with their estates without a reservation as to land being assigned for their support, it was not unusual for the new proprietor to leave them in possession of the land tilled with their own ploughs. For a time they might escape rent, but subsequently a low rate was put upon their lands, and these may still be recognised by the two facts, that (*a*) possession of the particular fields has seldom if ever changed, or if there has been such change, that the original area is maintained; and (*b*) the rates are still below the rents of other persons of the same class. Where the lands have been changed, either as to locality or area, and where there is no special favour in the rates of rent as compared with others of the same caste, the subproprietary status has merged into that of cultivator. *Second*, it was usual to assign to the junior branches of a proprietary family certain lands for their support, instead of giving them the ancestral shares to which they were ordinarily entitled. Such appanages were also known by the name of *Sīr*.

(4.) *Nānkār.*—The only difference locally between this and *Dīdārī*, which has already been described, is that in the case of the latter, *land* was assigned after one of two methods; in the case of the former, a portion of the rental in *money* was assigned, according to either of the same two methods. When a fractional share of the rental was assigned as *Nānkār*, it was usually assumed on the rental of that time, and remained a fixed item, without being subject to future enhancement or curtailment. In very rare instances, however, it did happen that the *Nānkār* allowance was subject to annual adjustment, according to the result of the year's crop, the original extent of share assigned alone remaining fixed. The money is either paid over by the proprietor to the subproprietor, or the latter is allowed a remission equal to the amount in the rents of any lands he may hold as a cultivator. No instance has occurred in this settlement in which the under-proprietor was found to be in the enjoyment of both a money allowance and of *sīr* land.

(5.) *Shankalap.*—In practice the procedure of the native rule was different where a whole village, on the one hand, or certain lands on the other, were held under this tenure. In the former case a sum was paid down under mutual arrangement, and a deed was prepared, making over the village as a subtenure at favoured rates. In the latter case the poorer outlying or uncultivated lands were generally made over for a money consideration, of which a portion was to be cultivated, subject to the payment of rent, and the rest was left rent-free on account of village site, groves, &c. In rare instances a few arable *bīghas* were also specially allowed to be retained rent-free. In these cases the principle of the tenure, as mutually arranged, was that the cultivated portion only of the grant was to be subjected to the graduated enhancement of rent, till a fixed maximum amount was reached, in a given number of years.

(6.) *Birt.*—The distinction between purchased *Birts* and purchased *Shankalaps* is locally, at all events, quite infinitesimal. Neither tenure is, as has been so often erroneously supposed, confined exclusively to Brahmans, although undoubtedly fewer of the inferior castes have been found holding purchased *Shankalaps* than holding purchased *Birts.* As a matter of fact, Mohammedan proprietors and European grantees have been known to dispose of both of these land-improving tenures, proof positive that Hindu superstition had necessarily little to do with their origin.

We take the following account of the *Birt* tenures of the sub-Himalayan districts, from the *Calcutta Review* of 1866 :—
"These tenures, under the native rule, were invariably *subordinate;* that is, the holders, as expressed by Mr Thomason, were 'non-proprietary, from not being in direct engagement with the Government.' There were various phases of the tenure, but without exception such rights had their origin in the owner of the land. The two most marked kinds were the *purchased Birt* and the *conferred Birt.* The *first,* conveyed a subordinate title for ever, and the right has therefore been acknowledged and judicially decreed by the Oudh Settlement Courts. The last was eleemosynary, and, according to general usage, pending the donor's pleasure only; it is therefore for the holder to establish that, by local custom, he had a recognisable right.

"The incidence of the recognised *Birt* sub-tenure varies in almost every estate, but the most common feature is, that a landlord, being in want of money, or wishing to have waste-land brought under the plough, assigns a certain portion of land to a Brahman or other individual, on the latter advancing him a sum of money. An annual rent in perpetuity, perhaps a low one, is generally fixed at the time, or it is arranged that a part of the land shall for ever remain rent free, and the rest of it shall be subject to future enhancement at the will of the donor; but whatever the special conditions may be, the essence of the whole transaction is, that a subproprietary, and not a proprietary, title is conveyed, and that, according to immemorial usage, the *Birt* tenure remained in the parent estate as before. We are not quite clear how far the *perpetuity* clause, in such agreements as these, was respected under the native rule, or whether the sub-tenure continued to exist at all after the donor, his sons, and perhaps his grandsons, had died off. We rather think the tenure vanished with these; but of one thing we are well satisfied, and that is, that nothing beyond a *sub-tenure* was ever intentionally conveyed under a *Birt* deed.

"The former procedure in the older provinces was very different to this. There the superior owner was altogether deprived of his proprietary title, which again was transferred to the *Birt* holder, the settlement being made with the latter, subject to a money charge of 20 per cent. in excess of the Government demand, which sum, after realisation in the usual way, the Government handed over to the ousted proprietor from its own treasury, under the euphonious name of compensation.

"By the Oudh procedure, the transformation is one in designation only; for the tallukdār will be upheld in the possession of his superior rights and interests as formerly enjoyed, whilst the subproprietor's tenure will with equal care be protected, and he will be maintained by us in the unfettered control of his land, provided that he pays the tallukdār the rent which is determined by the settlement officer. This rent will ordinarily be the same as that previously paid under the native rule, except where such previous rent falls short of the revised Government demand, in which case it will be raised to the amount of the Government demand, *plus* 5 per cent. This percentage to the tallukdār is the sterile and only remuneration allowed to him in such cases for fulfilling the by no means sinecure office of *buffer* between the subproprietor and the native officers of Government, whereby the smaller holder is saved both money and inconvenience, in that most unpopular of all proceedings, viz., the payment of rent.

"But in the case of the older provinces, the Law of Limitations notwithstanding, all rights of property were disregarded; and without reference to the fact that rent-rolls, under our rule, were daily improving in a country then notoriously sparsely populated, no more than 20 per cent., calculated on the rent-rolls of that backward period, was fixed by Government as full compensation for the loss of superior rights, and handed over to those who had been thus deprived of them. This compensation, moreover, was not given in perpetuity, for it has recently been cut down to 10 per cent., and the result is apparent in the circumstance that the dispossessed Rājās of the old ceded districts are Rājās in name only, while each subproprietary *Birtia* has developed into a hereditary zamīndār.

"It may be mentioned that in the older provinces, under the Settlement of IX. of 1833, no attempt was made to discriminate between a *purchased* and a *conferred* Birt title. The man who had paid money for his hereditary title, and the man who got his tenure as a mere wound-pension for life, or while he continued to dust out the family chapel, was alike converted into a full proprietor."

(7.) *Bai-kitat.*—Many instances could be given in which fields or patches of land have been sold by the proprietor in subordinate tenure, under specific agreement, for agricultural purposes. The status of the subproprietor in these cases has been secured, and does not differ much from the *Birt* and *Shankalap* purchaser. No distinctive local name has been found for this class of sub-tenures.

(8.) *Baghat.*—Groves have been found to be of four classes. Belonging to (1) the present proprietor of the village; (2) the former proprietors; (3) the *Shankalapdārs* and *Birtdārs*, and (4) the tenants-at-will. The first of these are of course part and parcel of the owner's property; the second and third classes pertain to subordinate tenures. In all these three classes, the existing right, superior or subordinate, as the case may be, extends to both the land and the trees. The fourth class of groves has its origin in verbal arrangements entered into by the subproprietor and his cultivators. The rights of the latter in such orchards extend to eating the fruit, gathering the dry wood, and cutting down trees for home use, in roofing a house, making farm implements and the like. The tenure ordinarily ends on the cultivator leaving the village and giving up his farm. He could not replace the trees if they were removed without the special permission of his superior. The landlord takes no rent for grove-lands, but he can claim fruit on festive occasions, and he might fell a tree if he required the wood.

(9.) *Biswī.*—(*a*) When a whole village or entire fractional holding was mortgaged under native rule, it was usual for the mortgagee to obtain both possession of the land, and engagement direct with the Government for the revenue. Occasionally, however, the mortgagee obtained possession only without direct engagement; and in such case, after deducting his interest from the assumed rental, he paid the estimated difference in the shape of a quit-rent to the mortgagor, under the name of *parmsānā*. During revision of settlement, in cases in which redemption could no longer be allowed under existing rules, the mortgagee has invariably been declared to be the proprietor. (*b*) In the case of lands less in extent than a fractional portion of a village, such holdings under the native Government always remained attached to the parent village. The gross rental of such lands was assumed at the time of the transaction; the interest of the loan was then deducted from the item so assumed, and the difference, called *parmsānā*, was the quit-rent to be paid by the mortgagee to the mortgagor. The instances in which no such quit-rent was fixed were rare. In either case the mortgagor paid the Government demand. The former universal custom and condition as to re-entry was, that repayment of the loan might always be made at the end of any season, when the crops were off the ground; but our procedure has been in accordance with the ruling that in such cases the twelve-year limitation rule is to be applied, counting from the time when either party set the conditions of the original agreement aside; and where redemption cannot follow, the mortgagee is decreed an intermediate title, subject to the payment of the Government demand, *plus* 5 per cent. Claims of mortgagees out of possession have either been treated as money debts, owing to possession never having been transferred under existing rules; or if possession had actually followed the transaction, it was restored, if the special conditions had been infringed, and if the dispossession was within the limitation mentioned in the penultimate paragraph.

It now remains to be observed, that at the outset of our judicial work proprietors were specially called upon to file lists of (1) all intermediate holders whom they meant to recognise, and (2) those whose pretensions they meant to refute; and this, in course of time, they did. Lists of those who were supposed to have intermediate rights were also required from the native Government officials. Each presiding officer was further required to keep a Register, in which were entered all allusions that might be made to *Sīr* or *Dīdārī* tenures in the course of investigating proprietary or subproprietary tenures. With the help of precautions such as these, the position of many intermediate holders has, it is hoped, been secured, who might hereafter have suffered by remaining for the time silent.

In the disposal of intermediate claims, great pains were taken to induce the parties to endeavour to come to terms amongst themselves. Where they came to an adjustment, the conditions were at once reduced to writing, and a decree by consent was briefly recorded. Where the issues were confined to narrow limits, the parties were exhorted to compromise, and any of their friends who might be in attendance were desired to aid them in so doing; and it was only when these means failed that contested cases were disposed of in the Faizabad Settlement Courts. The relief that has resulted to the parties themselves, and to the presiding officers, from this procedure, is incalculable, and the subject has been on different occasions favourably noticed by the Chief Commissioner, and by the Government of India.

During the currency of the Summary Settlement, the

litigation between the different classes connected with the soil has been exceptionally great in this quarter; and it was by no means uncommon for the same cause to be brought forward under a variety of different phases, as, for instance, first as an ouster case, then as an adjustment-of-rent case, and lastly, as a suit for arrears of rent, the issue underlying the whole matter being the status of the inferior holder. In such cases the latter was harassed by constant attendance at Court, while the landlord was kept out of his rent, although he still had to make good his own revenue. The experience gained during these bitter years of contention has had the effect of facilitating our endeavours to bring about compromises during the revision of settlement. Both parties have had enough of law; they have learnt to perceive that they must still both remain attached to the soil, and they have therefore found it to be to their mutual interest to listen to reason, and to arrange such terms, based on the proportion of profits formerly enjoyed by them respectively, as could be accepted by either side with equal advantage. In a large proportion of cases the parties have adjusted their payments amongst themselves. When this was not done, the procedure has varied thus:—(1) In all low-rated or rent-free holdings, retained in virtue of former proprietary rights, the *status quo ante* has been perpetuated; and (2) in all other intermediate holdings future payments have been determined with advertance to, *first*, the merits of each case, and *second*, the Government demand now fixed.

Referring now to the distribution of profits in lands that have been sub-settled, it has been found impossible in all cases to abide strictly by the letter of the rule officially prescribed; because, before it could be literally carried out, it was necessary that the king's demand on every village should be known. The fact is, the instances were rare in which this information was forthcoming. Where it was found, the rule was of course followed. Where it was not found, the plan described in the following quotation was substituted:—

"The ascertaining of a tallukdār's profit from any village of his estate is contingent on discovering what he paid to Government for such village. The profit of the subproprietor can be ascertained; *e.g.*, having found the gross rental, and deducted therefrom the sum that the subproprietor paid to the proprietor, what is left may be assumed to be the profit of the former. So if the subproprietor's rent, and the gross rental of the king's time can be discovered, the difference between the two sums was his profit at that time, and he will be entitled to a similar proportion now, subject, however, to certain conditions, viz.—

"(1.) If the gross rental is the same now as in the king's time, the *status quo* of that period should be maintained.

"(2.) If by the exertion of the subproprietor the gross rental of the village has increased, the amount of increase should be separated from the original gross rental, and the subproprietor's share of the latter first determined. Then as to the amount of the increase, after deducting therefrom 51¼ per cent. as the share of the Government, *plus* 5 per cent. for the superior's risk and trouble, whatever remains should be added to the subproprietor's profit. In this case the improvement having been effected by the subproprietor, he alone is entitled to the full benefit, and the result will perhaps be better understood by illustration, thus:—

VILLAGE RAMPUR.	KING'S TIME.		REVISED ASSESSMENT.		
	Rs.	Rs.		Rs.	Rs.
Gross rental, .	...	800	Gross rental, .	...	900
Subproprietor used to pay, .	600	} 800	Subproprietor will now pay,	653.12	} 900
and received,	200		and receive, .	246.4	

"It will be seen that the gross rental has here increased Rs. 100. Of that sum 51¼ per cent., or Rs. 51, 4a., will go as revenue to Government, 5 per cent. on that sum, or Rs. 2, 8a., to the superior holder, making the subproprietor's payment Rs. 53, 12a., and leaving him on an increased profit of Rs. 46, 4a.

"(3.) But if the gross rental has increased by the exertions of the proprietor, and independently of the subproprietor, then the former will derive all the profit; or, to return to our illustration, the subproprietor will be entitled to no more than the Rs. 200 which he formerly received.

"(4.) If the profits have increased independently of the exertions of either party, and this is due solely to the march of civilisation, the enhanced rental will be shared proportionally with reference to what they enjoyed formerly. In other words, and keeping our illustration still in view, the gross rental under a powerful Government having increased from Rs. 800 to Rs. 900, without proprietary or subproprietary exertion, the intermediate holder will now get Rs. 223, 2a., and his superior Rs. 676, 14a. In this instance we have to make the same deductions as before, and the same increase of profit remains, viz., Rs. 46, 4a. This has to be divided equally, each party receiving Rs. 23, 2a.

"(5.) Instances will arise in which the gross rental has increased by the process of assessing the *Sīr* land of subproprietors according to capabilities, which was in the king's time entered in the rent-rolls at low rates. But such enhancement is a mere matter of account in connection with the assessment of the Government demand, and the sub-proprietor will reap the full advantage as heretofore, the calculations being made, as in the second instance given above, when the improvement had been effected by the subproprietor solely."

Nothing more remains to be said of proprietary or sub-proprietary tenures. A few words may, however, be added, on the position of certain parties whose occupancy is not based on inherent right, but on the will of the proprietor, such as (1) old cultivators, (2) Māfidārs, (3) Marwatdārs, and (4) Jāegīrdārs. In regard to the first of these classes, it was determined, after prolonged inquiry, the results of which are shown in Chapter III. of this book, that they were without rights which could be maintained in opposition to the wishes of the proprietor. Referring to the second class, *māfi* grants were often made by proprietors to Brahmans, Bhāts, Fakīrs, &c., in connection with their religious services and prejudices. They were purely eleemosynary, generally hereditary, never transferable. Resumption of such grants was unusual, even when the property changed hands. When pressure was put on the proprietor, he might for a time assess such grants; but with the withdrawal of the necessity the payments generally ceased. Instances are, however, not unknown, in which the proprietors lightly assessed such holdings permanently. *Marwat* grants are neither more nor less than pensions given to the heirs of retainers killed in the service of the proprietor, in the shape of a little rent-free land; while *jāegīrs* are lands given to retainers still in service, in lieu of wages. At first, claims to these various sorts of grants were not cognisable in the Settlement Department; but the more recent procedure has been to dispose of them in accordance with a well-established local custom.

CHAPTER II.

FURTHER REMARKS ON PROPRIETARY AND SUBPROPRIETARY TENURES; (AN OFFICIAL MEMORANDUM).

REFERRING to the terms, *pukhtā*, *pukhtadāri*, and holding under *pukhtā* or *pakkā* lease, the tenure to which they apply is undoubtedly to be recognised by the fact, that after paying the demand, which must be a fixed lump sum, the profit or loss pertains to the engagement-holder (*kabūliyutdār*), whether he makes the collections or not. It is not absolutely necessary that he should personally collect the rents, as will be seen from the following instances:—

First, When he had difficulty in collecting the rents, owing to the recusancy of the tenants, it was usual for the engagement-holder to seek the aid of the Government officials, who thereon appointed a man called a *jamōgdār* to make the collections, and debit them to the revenue of the engagement-holder. If the full amount of the Government demand was not thus realised, the engagement-holder and his surety were as fully responsible for the balance as if the former had remained in rent-collecting possession; he was also responsible for all the expenses of the temporary collector and his establishment. This system of *jamōg* was neither more nor less than what our Revenue Officers know by the term *kūrk-tehsīl* as defined in paragraphs 72 to 76 of the "Directions" for their guidance. The above remarks describe the *volun-*

tary jamōg system, but it was usual for the Government authorities to adopt the same plan when they had, or assumed that they had, reason to apprehend default on the part of the engagement-holder. This, of course, as far as the latter's wishes were concerned, was *involuntary.*

Second, It was very usual for engagement-holders to have the amount of their revenue assigned by Government to some of its military servants in lieu of their pay, and the Nāzim then debited the amount to the pay of the regiment to which such servants belonged, under what was known as the *kabz* system. In such case the military officer (kabzdār) used to depute his own collector (jamōgdār) to act for him, the engagement-holder (kabūliyutdār) being responsible for all expenses.

Third, It was also very common for the engagement-holder to nominate a surety (mālzāmin) for the amount of his revenue, and in this case the collections were assigned to the latter, in the capacity of *jamōgdār.* Bonds used to be executed under which the surety became responsible to Government, and the engagement-holder to the surety.

In each of these three instances the engagement-holder did not collect the rents, but he was nevertheless known to hold the village *pakkā,* and to be solely interested in the profit or loss. It was also quite possible for the zamīndār to be in rent-collecting possession of the village, and yet for the village to be the opposite of *pakka,* that is *kachcha.* This often happened when the zamīndār declined to pay the assessment fixed upon the village, and the profits were too small to meet the expenses of a regular collecting (*jamōg*) establishment. In such case the Government officials were in the habit of making over the collections to the zamīndār out of engagement, taking an agreement from him to pay the full amount realised into the Government Treasury. No responsibility rested in this case with the zamīndār to make good any difference between the sum collected and the sum for which he declined to enter into engagements. In lieu of his labour, however, he was permitted to retain the same personal allowance (nankār) as he enjoyed while he held the village under regular engagement; and he was also left in rent-free possession of any *sīr* land that he may have tilled with his own stock at the time that he relinquished his engagement. These details pertain to the arrangements entered into between the Government officials and the proprietors or engagement-holders of estates. I now proceed to consider the relations that existed between proprietors and subproprietors under the native rule.

It was common for proprietors to apply the system of *jamōg*, as I have above described it, to their subordinate proprietors, in regard to *pakkā* villages, in much the same manner as the Government officials applied it to themselves. But their procedure was perfectly different in regard to *kachcha* villages. In the case of the latter the ex-proprietors were only employed to make the collections when they happened to have accepted the service, civil or military, of the proprietor, and they then had to account for the full amount collected, receiving their pay as a remission. If such servants were in possession of *sīr*, *nankār*, or other ex-proprietary perquisites, prior to their being intrusted by the proprietor with the duty of collecting the rents, it was continued to them in addition to the remission, in lieu of wages.

There was this marked difference between the conduct of

the Government officials on the one hand, and the proprietors on the other, in regard to holding land under direct management, viz., that as an invariable rule, the *former* allowed the proprietor out of engagement to retain his *sīr* and *nankār* under any circumstances; while it was, it may be said, quite exceptional for the *latter* to allow the ex-proprietor, out of village management, to continue to hold his *sīr* and *nankār*. On a full consideration of all these circumstances, it may be yielded that it is perfectly correct to hold that person to be in possession of the village who receives the profits, and is responsible for the loss.

Under the native Government the words *pukhtā* and *pukhtadāri* were unknown; they are a recent creation of those who use our own stilted *Kachahri* phraseology. In former days, when an *ex-proprietor* leased his village for a fixed sum, he was said to hold it *pakkā*, whether any of those rights, which we now define as *subproprietary*, were reserved by him or not. On the other hand, if a *stranger* leased the village, the transaction was invariably designated an *ijara*, or as *mustājiri*, and never as *pakkā*. The word *thīkā* was rarely, if ever, used before our time. The words *pakkā* and *kachcha* were always used under the king's government antithetically, and they must be held to have had a direct connection with former *rights*, because, as has already been shown, if a stranger leased, he did not hold, *pakkā*. If there were no rights, there would have been no use for the antithetical word *kachcha*; and it therefore follows, that where the two words *pakkā* and *kachcha* are found in use, more than a farming or leasing tenure is at stake. There is in the minds of the claimants of subproprietary tenures a vast distinction between *pakkā* and *thīkā*. By the former word they unmistakably mean what we have now designated a *pukhtadāri* tenure; but the rendering which they would have us to accept is wrong, the correct meaning being that which I have already above given.

So much for *subproprietary* tenures. I now proceed to remark upon *proprietary* rights. The views of one of our most distinguished Oudh Settlement officers, Captain ——, on this last tenure, are thus abstracted:—(1.) The zamīndār either held the engagement direct of his village, or Government officials managed it direct; or the ex-zamīndār held his village *pakkā*, paying to a tallukdār, or the latter held it Kachcha. In any one of these four cases the zamīndār's profit consisted in the remission that it was the custom to allow from the gross rental under the name of *nankār*, and also the *sīr* land or home farm held at low rates, or, it may be, rent-free. (2.) It was entirely at the disposal of the tallukdār to lease the village at a lump sum to the ex-zamīndār, or to make the collections direct, and it was not considered unjust or oppressive by the latter for the tallukdār, at his pleasure, to adopt this last course. (3.) Notwithstanding that the village may always have been held pakkā by the old zamīndārs, new outlying hamlets (*pūrwas*) were always established (by strangers, I presume is meant) under the *sanad* of the tallukdār. (4.) In the subproprietary decrees for villages now being issued in favour of these old zamīndārs, rights are being created which did not exist under the native rule, contrary to the provisions of Lord Canning's *sanad*. For if the village is decreed in subproprietary tenure, everything contained within its demarcated bounds is covered by the decree, although it may have been the case that, under the native rule, the subproprietor, for a long series of years, had no concern with nine-tenths of what the decree now gives him.

I am of opinion that these premises are erroneous, and in order that the real state of the case may be made apparent, it is necessary, in the first place, that the former method of assessing the Government demand and the *nankār* allowance of the proprietor should be understood. The Nāzim invariably fixed the Government demand. His powers in this respect were final when he farmed his charge. If he, on the other hand, simply managed it on the part of Government, his proposals required the confirmation of the Minister. No rule existed under which the gross rental was estimated, a fixed portion being set aside for the state, and the residue for the proprietor. The Nāzims called on the Kānūngos to file lists of estates for past years (usually ranging from ten to twenty), showing the demand of those years, and on this data the Nāzim determined the revenue of the year, which then, in most instances, remained unaltered during his term of office. If he was clever, and well-supported at the capital, he fixed a comparatively high demand; otherwise, he had to be satisfied with accepting the revenue of former years. In rare instances, if the demand on an estate was largely increased, or if the proprietor raised the question of deteriorated assets, a Kānūngo used to be deputed to make a rough estimate or valuation (*shūdkār*) on the spot, and upon this, when considered necessary, something was struck off the former demand. Under all circumstances, the demand fixed by the Nāzim was the maximum sum that it was considered possible for the estate to pay; but it must be borne in mind that the *real* "jamā" was that which was actually collected.

The remission from their revenue known as *Nankār-i-dehī* was a privilege common to most zamīndārs. But it was not an inherent right of proprietorship; it was allowed, without exception, to all tallukdārs, and it may be assumed that 90 per cent. of the smaller proprietors also enjoyed it, while the remainder did not. The following account has been furnished to me of the origin of the tenure; but nankār was known at a still more remote period. In the time of Akbar, proprietors, as such, enjoyed a drawback of two per cent. by the name of *sud-doi* (literally, two in a hundred). When Safdar Jang was *Wazīr* of the Empire, he also retained the subadārship of Oudh and Allahabad; he had his headquarters at Delhi, and managed Oudh through his deputy, Raja Newal Rāi. In the war that followed, the Nawab of Farakhabād slew Newal Rāi at Kanoj, and conquered Oudh. Safdar Jang hastened to retake Oudh, and to propitiate the landed proprietors; remissions of revenue, of greater or less extent, according to the influence of the parties, were freely granted. To these was then given the name of *nankār*, and the term *sud-doi* has since fallen out of use.

This description of nankār is locally known as of two kinds, (1) Nankar-san-Baīs, and (2) Kami-rakūmāt. During the reigns of Asf-ūd-daula and his predecessors, the revenues of the state were sadly eaten into by these remissions and rent-free grants; most of these, as is well known, were resumed by Nawab Sādat Ali under the excellent revenue arrangements which he inaugurated. After his death the office of Nazim was farmed by different parties, and the utmost looseness of practice, as regards granting nankār remissions, prevailed until the year 1247 Fasli, when Shaf-Shikam Khan was appointed Nāzim on the *amānut*, or direct system, and the rule was then laid down by the Government that those remissions only were to be recognised which Sādut Ali had left unresumed in his settlement of 1222 Fasli. But in practice, that Nāzim respected alike the nankārs allowed in that year, and also those granted by subsequent Nāzims down to his own day. He, however, maintained the distinction in the accounts where the two descriptions were separately shown, and where his accounts were submitted for audit at Lucknow, they were passed, the remissions of 1222 Fasli and previous years under the name of Nankār-sun-Baīs and those of subsequent years, not, it will be observed, as nankār, but as kami-rakūmāt. The method of collecting and adjusting these different remissions between the Nāzim and the proprietors was as follows:—The nankār of 1222 Fasli was debited to the Government as so much money realised. In the case of the other description, the amount of the demand was entered; from that the remissions were deducted, and the balance was the *actual* Government demand. It may facilitate the comprehension to reduce this to figures, as follows:—

NANKĀR OF 1222 FASLI.		KAMI-RAKŪMĀT.	
Government demand, .	Rs. 500	Government demand, .	Rs. 500
Realised, ...	300	Kami-rakūmāt, . .	100
Balance, ...	200	Paying juma . . .	400
Deduct nankār of 1222 Fasli, ...	100		
Still due, ...	100		

So that in the one case the remission is allowed as an actual payment; and in the other it is entered as a reduction from the sum that it is the avowed intention to collect.

A reason has already been assigned as to why the nankār remissions of 1222 Fasli came originally to be allowed; it may now be stated that the other remissions were granted to proprietors on account of such services as presenting themselves and attending upon the Nāzim, agreeing to enhancements of revenue, &c., and such items, were struck off the amount which the Nāzim had to pay to the Government for farming the office.

Of course the Government had the power of veto; but so long as the Nāzim was in friendly relations with the Ministers of State, this power was never exercised. When such remissions had once been audited at Lucknow, in the Nāzim's annual accounts, they became so far permanent that it was quite exceptional for future Nāzims to resume them. When such resumptions did, however, take place, redress could not be obtained at Lucknow, because there such remissions were not looked upon as being held under any actual right. In neither of these kinds of remissions was any system of percentage or proportion followed.

When it has thus been made evident that the Government revenue and the proprietary remission were fixed and determined upon no known rule or principle of computation, it cannot be laid down that the zamīndār's rights consisted solely in the possession of his *nankār* and *sīr*. Accepting for the sake of argument Captain ——'s exposition of the question as correct, can it be believed that in those estates, and they are numerous, where the proprietor enjoyed no nankār allowance, his rights consisted in no more than the few acres of *sīr*, constituting the home farm, on which alone he was dependent for support? But I cannot accept this position as correct. The fact is, no attempt was ever made, under the native rule, to define how much of the gross produce should go to the State and how much to the proprietors. Although it may be established that under direct [management the zamīndār got no more than the profit arising out of his *sīr* and *nankār*, it must not on this account be considered as proved that these constituted the sole rights of the zamīndār. The system under which Nāzims held khām, leaving the proprietors their nankār and sīr, was very much akin to the process known to our own Revenue system as khām tehsīl, as explained in the "Directions," under which the profits are sequestered; and no rendering of accounts at the end of the operation is deemed necessary. The foregoing remarks apply especially to arrangements between the Government and the proprietors; we shall now turn to the relations that existed between the latter and their subproprietors.

When villages were incorporated into tallukas *without* purchase, and the possession of the late zamīndārs remained undisturbed, it was never the rule to set apart sīr, assign nankār, and fix the Government demand with any reference whatever to the gross rental. In these cases it was very much the custom for the tallukdār to let the ex-proprietor down gently by taking no more from him for a few years than the latter formerly paid to the State. He would afterwards by degrees screw up the demand, but never to such an extent that there should actually be no portion of the gross rental left to the ex-proprietors, and this, in addition to the sīr and sāir of the village: moreover, it was by no means the invariable rule for tallukdārs not to assess subproprietary sīr. It was of frequent occurrence for the holders of the latter to have to pay upon their sīr upon the well-known Bāchh principle; and this was more especially the case when the properties of communities, consisting of numerous members, were absorbed into tallukas, because in this class of cases it was by no means uncommon for the great majority of the cultivation, or perhaps the whole of it, to be held as sīr. In the cases of which we are speaking, viz., villages incorporated without purchase, instances would arise when the tallukdār had resort to direct management, and on such occasions he would allow the former proprietors (1) to hold all or some of their sīr at favourable rates; or (2) he would give them a small money allowance instead; or (3) it might be that he turned them out altogether, without showing them any consideration whatsoever.

In this class of unpurchased tenures it was far from the impression of former proprietors that it was a matter contingent solely on the will and pleasure of the tallukdār to hold *pakkā* or *khām* at his option; on the contrary, they believed that in all justice they had the most undeniable right themselves to hold *pakkā* under the tallukdār to the extent; and I know many instances in which the right was exercised, that they could even withdraw their village altogether from a talluka, and themselves engage for it direct with the Government, or include it in the rent-roll on similar terms of some other landowner. In such cases as these, how is it possible to say that the rights of the subproprietors under the native rule amounted to no more than the profits of their sīr and nankār? and on what principle of justice could we now confine their subproprietary interests to these perquisites alone?

Proceeding now to the consideration of villages held under purchase by tallukdārs, it will be found that in this class of cases the former proprietors have been treated in one of the two following ways: either they will have had some consideration shown them at the time of purchase, known locally as *dīdārī*, and which might be an annual allowance, or a certain portion of rent-free or low-rated land; or they have had no such consideration shown, and have been reduced to the status of tenants-at-will.

The conclusion to be drawn from the above particulars relating to villages absorbed into tallukas, whether by trust, force, purchase, or other means, is that it was not an invariable rule for the sīr and nankār of proprietors and subproprietors to be fixed and determined quantities. It follows, I think, that in estates incorporated under no valid tenure, and for which claims are advanced which are cognisable under the Law of Limitations, no injustice or breach of *sanad* is committed in decreeing a subproprietary status.

It would appear from Captain ——'s showing, that the area of mauzas in his district is very extensive, and they are very different in this respect from those of Faizabād. It would seem to be no uncommon thing for a village to have from ten to twenty hamlets attached to it, which have been from time to time settled by strangers on land that was badly cultivated or altogether waste, under the sanad, not of the former proprietors, but of the tallukdār. These hamlets, and the lands attached to them, are described as never having been under the management or control of the ex-proprietors, although they may all along have leased the parent village. It seems that the district procedure referred to is, supposing the subproprietary title to the parent village to be made out, to decree the said village as set up by the Demarcation Officer, as well as every hamlet contained within the demarcation boundaries, to the fortunate ex-zamīndār. And to this procedure Captain —— most naturally, I think, objects, on the ground that new rights are being daily created by such decrees, to the entire confusion of the tallukdārs' sanads. But I am not aware of any order under which this procedure is enjoined. The Demarcation Department adjusted no rights; they simply laid down the boundaries of villages according to possession as it was found to exist, leaving all questions of right to the Settlement Department; and as a result, many of their proceedings have been, and are being, reversed in this district, under the operation of decrees of the Settlement Courts, which has necessitated the reformation of a demarcated village into two or more distinct properties; and this is evidently what ought to be done, if it has not already been done in Captain ——'s district also. If a village has been decreed in subproprietary tenure, that decree should, of course, cover nothing that the subproprietor was not in possession of within the limitation period. If before February 1844 the tallukdār granted sanads under which hamlets were established by strangers, who paid the rents to the former, and not through the lease-holder of the parent village, the latter, in the event of his being decreed to be the subproprietor of such parent village, has no more to do with the hamlets established by the tallukdār than I have. They are the sole property of the tallukdār, to do with them as he chooses, subject to any conditions he may have made relative to their being established. If my ideas are correct, some revision of the decrees of the district in question will be necessary. It will not be necessary to demarcate separately any hamlets that may be found to be distinct property from the parent village, nor to have a separate field register and map, nor even to show them separately on the village map, because the existing orders are that *khateonis* are necesssary for *pakkā* villages in tallukas; these papers have therefore been already prepared for the parent villages of which I write, and they will answer all the purpose of identifying the fields that belong to the different integral portions.

CHAPTER III.

ON TENANT'S RIGHT OF OCCUPANCY (AN OFFICIAL REPORT).

A THOROUGH investigation into the rights of tenants having been completed, it embraces an inquiry into occupancy as it existed (1) in the Faizabad District when we annexed Oudh, and (2) in the adjoining district of Azimgarh prior to settlement under Regulation IX. of 1833. Dividing the subject into these two parts, I now proceed to detail our operations.

Part I. Three descriptions of cases have come under inquiry in the Faizabad District. First, Under the Financial Commissioner's *Circular* No. 2, of 1864, every cultivator in twenty-seven villages was called before the Settlement Officer or his assistant, and his status was inquired into. Second, Ten out of the thirteen applications made to the Settlement Courts, and referred to in the last *Annual Report*, were examined. Third, Under the Financial Commissioner's *Circular* No. 6, of 1864, nineteen applications made to the District Courts to hold possession of land as cultivators, contrary to the will of the proprietors, were inquired into.

Referring to the first of these three classes of cases, the twenty-seven villages examined embrace thirteen in tallukas and fourteen in non-tallukas, and they are spread over two tehsīl and six pargana subdivisions: in all of these no very marked difference in custom has been found to exist. The well-known distinction of high-caste (ashrāf) and low-caste (arzul) cultivators is found to exist, and favour is shown to the former, which includes Brahmans, Chhatris, and Kayaths, in their rents; but custom in this respect varies in almost every village, and in the majority of instances no such consideration is shown. It is a noteworthy fact that where this favour is shown, prescription, or length of occupancy, has nothing to do with the matter; because the ashrāf cultivator, who has occupied his land for a few weeks only, is found to be on precisely equal terms in this respect with the man who has cultivated his field for several lives. It is the fact of *residing in the village* that is the great desideratum with the zamīndār, as implying certainty that the fields will not only be cultivated, but to some extent manured, against the uncertainty and the absence of manure, that are the distinguishing features of the non-resident cultivator.

The consideration, where it exists, is shown by (1) a reduction in the rent of so much per bīgha of land, or (2) so much per rupee of rent. The amount of this reduction varies in every village, but in each village the recipients of the favour enjoy it in like proportion. In amount the reduction ranges from a maximum of six annas to a minimum of nine pies in the rupee. It must not be supposed that this favour in rent used to give any immunity from enhancement; for in the great majority of cases it has been found that the favoured rates were raised in precisely the same proportion as all the others, and in a few instances only was favour to a slight extent shown in the amount of enhancement. Where favour was shown on the bīgha principle, enhancement affected the recipient in precisely the same proportion as it did the ordinary cultivator; but where it was shown in the rupee, then the recipient gained a further advantage in the calculation. For instance A (the full payer) rents his field at Rs. 4, and B (the favoured payer) his at Rs. 3, 12a. An enhancement is made of an anna per rupee in the rents of all resident cultivators, and it affects the field of A to the extent of four annas, and of B of three annas and nine pies only; so that B having all along benefited by one reduction of four annas, derives the benefit of a second reduction of three pies. All other castes, except the three mentioned above, who alone have been found to be included in the *ashrāf*, pay at full rates. The present inquiry has fully established, that, as a matter of fact, cultivators, whether low-rated or otherwise, were rarely ousted under the native rule so long as they paid their rents; and there was the less necessity to exercise the right of ouster, since it was well known to all concerned that the right could not be resisted. The landlord raised his rent to what he considered the full value of the land; sometimes a single enhancement was equal to 50 per cent. on the former rent. He knew his interests well enough to stop short of driving away his tenants; and this knowledge being acted upon, the tenants generally agreed to his terms, and in this way things went on from one generation to another. Population was too limited to admit of competition for land, and in fact, much land lay waste. Under these circumstances, landlords had to search for and foster cultivators, and such a thing was unknown as one Asāmī outbidding another. All the cultivators who have been examined, with the sole exception of those of a single village, have freely admitted that in the king's time they had no rights, and they held, whether at full or at low rates, alike at the sole will and pleasure of the proprietor. Even in the exceptional village referred to, the low-caste cultivators also candidly admitted absence of all right as opposed to the will of the landlord. But besides these, there are fourteen Chhatri cultivators, holding at full rates, who alleged continuous possession at fixed rents, and who asserted a right to be maintained in their holdings so long as they paid their rents. The investigation that has now been made, has, however, quite disposed of their position; because it has been established (1) that their holdings varied in area, and (2) that their rents, which are equal in amount to those of all ordinary cultivators, have been subject to like enhancements with them. Instances have been found of the descendants of former owners living in the village and supporting themselves by agriculture or by service; they either pay full rates, like ordinary cultivators, or they are shown just the same amount of favour by reason of caste as is enjoyed by any other high-caste cultivator who may happen to be so privileged in the village.

In one village the *Ujāniā* Rājpūts were the former proprietors, and some of them are now found to be mere cultivators; they alleged a right to be maintained in possession of their fields so long as they continued to pay "a fair rent," but the existence of no right has been established. On the contrary, it has been elicited (1) that they had the same favour in rates by virtue of high caste as other non-proprietary high-caste cultivators, and no more; and (2) that their rents were raised precisely in the same manner as those of other respectable residents. Moreover, it was established (3) that some of these ex-proprietary cultivators had, of their own voluntary action, *relinquished* portions of the land they had long held at the favoured rates alluded to, instead of *transferring* them for a valuable consideration, which they would have done had vested interests been involved; and also (4) that the tallukdār had the power, and had exercised it, of curtailing when he liked some of these favoured holdings. Lastly, it was shown (5) that when such a cultivator died, his land was not divided by his representatives according to ancestral share, as is the invariable rule when rights of any kind in landed property are inherited, but according to the means of individual heirs to carry on the cultivation, as mutually determined between such heirs and the proprietor of the village: and all these five positions are alike obnoxious to the existence of any tenant right of occupancy.

Again, in one village, the parent one of the once powerful *Sakarwār* clan of Rājpūts, members of the ex-proprietary community remained in the service of the tallukdār as armed retainers till annexation, obtaining a remission of their rent as cultivators in lieu of wages. Since that time some of these men have been dismissed, their services being no longer required, and their land has been assessed at full market rates. One man has died, and his land has been resumed by the proprietor. These ex-proprietary cultivators allege that when their property was originally taken into the talluka, they applied for a *jīwan-birt* tenure for their support, but it was not allowed. Those of the community who chose to accept service obtained it, and in lieu of wages land was assigned to them, in some instances in one of the villages of their ancestral property, and in other instances in villages with which they had no former concern. The present inquiry has satisfactorily established that there is no direct connection between these service tenures as we found them existing, and the lost proprietary status of the holders; because (1) the acceptance of service of these persons was not in all cases simultaneous with the incorporation of the village in the talluka, members of the family having joined the service at various subsequent periods, when it suited their convenience to do so; (2) the service tenures were not given with any reference to the relative former position or extent of shares of the different coparceners in the village; and (3) the members of the community alone who accepted the service, individually derived the benefit of the land assigned in lieu of wages, and their former co-sharers, who held aloof, did not participate in any way therein. These three positions are alike obnoxious to the existence of any right of occupancy; and, as a matter of fact, a majority of the holders who were examined eventually admitted in Court that they held their service lands at the sole will and pleasure of the proprietor. In all other villages the ex-proprietary cultivators, without exception, admitted that they owed their position to the favour of the landlord of the day; and the inquiry has established beyond a doubt that there was no difference whatever between the status of these men and that of the ordinary non-proprietary cultivator.

Referring now to the *second* class of cases, viz., the thirteen claims to occupancy rights commented upon in last year's Settlement Report, it is a noteworthy fact that of these applicants twelve are residents of the Azimgarh, and the remaining one of the Jaunpūr border. And this is the whole secret of their coming forward. They hoped and believed that the tenant-right procedure of the adjoining provinces would be extended to Oudh, and they therefore lodged their claims. Ten of the thirteen cases have been investigated; the others I have not yet been able to get into Court. In nine of these the plaintiff admitted absence of all right under the native rule, and they assigned the change of Government as the sole reason for coming forward: five of the ten were new, and five were old cultivators; three of the ten at once withdrew their claims, and all ten were alike dismissed, no right of occupancy being proved.

Referring now to the *third* class of cases, viz., the claims of those who had petitioned the District Courts to be maintained in possession in opposition to the will of the proprietor, nineteen of these have been investigated, and, as a rule, the plaintiffs in all of them affirmed as their reason for coming forward the belief that the British Government maintained the *status quo* of every person who had any connection whatever with the soil. Of these nineteen persons five were recent cultivators; that is, their occupancy commenced within the period of our limitation laws, and the others were of old standing: the claims have all been alike dismissed, as no right of occupancy, as based on custom under the king's government, was established.

These proceedings indisputably establish to my mind that under the native rule there was no recognised right of occupancy. No one ever heard of such a claim being brought forward, or listened to, in any tribunal, authorised or otherwise. It cannot be said that this was owing to bad government, or owing to absence of the means of redress; because the same objection would apply just as much to claims for all other rights in land, such as used to be abundantly brought before the native officials, through our Military, or Residency, or the Court influence. Such cases are also known to have been frequently settled by arbitration; or finally, failing all other means of redress, the form of duress, known as *dharna*, and faith-renunciation, self-mutilation, or suicide, were often resorted to by those who had lost their rights. But a vigilant inquiry, extending over many weeks, has failed to bring to light a single instance of a person having recourse to any of these modes of redress, because he imagined that his occupancy amounted to a right which had in any way been interfered with.

To conclude the first part of this subject: when several hundreds of cultivators are, one may say, unanimous in asserting that they were never aware of being possessed of any right under the native Government, when it is shown that in no single instance, of the many that have come under inquiry, was subdivision of the holding of an old cultivator between his heirs made, according to the rule which invariably guides the partition of inherited rights in India, the conclusion appears to me to be perfectly irresistible that the former custom of the country recognised no such thing as a tenant's right of occupancy.

Part II. Having now given the result of the investigations into tenant occupancy in this district, I proceed to answer, by anticipation, a question which certainly will occur to most people, "How is it that the Settlement Officer of Faizabad can find no cultivators' rights, when the Settlement Officer of Azimgarh did find them, the two districts having, in fact, been one at the beginning of the century, when both were under native rule?" Having attentively studied all the available books of reference touching on the subject, and having also instituted inquiries of intelligent persons still living, who took part in the settlement proceedings of the bordering districts thirty years ago, the fact seems to me undeniable that no right of occupancy, apart from ex-proprietorship, existed even in Azimgarh, until our system created it. We acquired what are termed the Ceded Provinces, including the bordering districts of Azimgarh and Gorakhpūr, from the Oudh Government, under the treaty of 1801. We inaugurated our rule by the issue of a proclamation on the 15th July 1802, setting forth the principles upon which the settlement of the new territory was to be effected. This proclamation, somewhat modified, was subsequently enacted as Sec. 29, Reg. XXV. of 1803; and turning to it we find that the only reference it makes to the class of cultivators, is in laying down the rule that all *abwābs*, or miscellaneous extra charges, were in future to be included under the common denomination of rent, and that the granting of written leases by all parties who entered into engagements for the revenue with Government to their "dependent tallukdārs, raīyats, and under-tenants," was declared obligatory. Furthermore, Section 35 of the same regulation reserved to the Governor-General in council the power to enact other regulations, "for the protection and welfare of raīyats and cultivators of the soil."

This was followed, in the same year, by the enactment of Regulation XXX.,* prescribing rules for the exchange of

* "*Summary of the Old Law,*" *vide Mr Muir's minute of the* 29*th May* 1863.

Sec. 10, Reg. LI. of 1795, for Banāras, states that khudkāsht, or chhapparband raīyats cannot be dispossessed so long as they pay their rent at pargana rates.

Cl. 7, sec. 32, Reg. XXVIII. of 1803, provides for the case of tenants having the right of occupancy so long as a certain rent, or a rent determined on certain principles, according to local rates and usages, is paid.

Cl. 3, sec. 11, Reg. VIII. of 1819, and Sec. 32, Reg. IX. of 1822, recognise "khudkāsht, or resident and hereditary cultivators," or kadīmi raīyats, as not liable to ejectment; and so also Acts XII. of 1841, and I. of 1845, cl. 3, sec. 27.

Reg. VII. of 1822, cl. 1, sec. 9, directs the registration in the written leases, allowing the proprietors full power to do as they liked with their lands, "consistently with the rights of dependent tallukdārs, raīyats, or other descriptions of under-tenants and cultivators of the soil." The engagements were to be specific in their conditions, and, in case of dispute as to rates, that was to be disposed of by the District Civil Court "according to the rates established in the pargana for lands of the same description, or according to the legal and established rights of the parties, whether the same be ascertainable by written engagement, or defined by the laws and regulations, or upon general or local usage, which may be proved to have existed from time immemorial; this regulation not being meant to define or limit the actual rights of any description of landlords or tenants, which can be properly ascertained and determined by judicial investigation only." The same regulation provided that "mukurriridārs, istīmrārdārs, or other descriptions of under-tenants of land," who, "on the 10th November 1801, shall have been entitled to hold their tenures at a fixed annual rent, and shall have actually held the same at a fixed invariable amount for twelve complete years before that period," were not liable to

paper of village rights of cultivators, "whether possessing the right of hereditary occupancy or not."

The Regulations have from the first "taken for granted" a class of hereditary cultivators, and the Civil Courts were supposed to decide on the merits according to local custom.—Sec. 32, Reg. XXVIII. of 1803 (Mr Muir's, para. 11).

The rule enjoined under the Settlement of XI. of 1833 was to record in the khationi every cultivating holding under the denomination of proprietary, hereditary, non-hereditary, or service; but the Sudr Board's printed Circulars laid down no rule to discriminate hereditary from non-hereditary raīyats; it was simply provided that disputes were to be referred to arbitration, or decided by the collector; and the "Directions" are no more explicit.

"enhancement." Such persons had "clearly to establish that by the conditions of their tenures they were not liable to any increase of rent, and that they actually paid a fixed invariable annual rent during the above period" (Sec. 12). But these persons are afterwards explained to be holders under grant of preceding Governments, and not what we now call *cultivators* at all. (See Reg. I. of 1815; Sec. 4, Reg. II. of 1819; and Sec. 17, Reg. VII. of 1822). We in Oudh, in fact, recognise them as a superior class, viz., *sub-proprietors.*

The next important Regulation bearing on the relations of landlord and tenant is V. of 1812, but it seems confined to lands managed for the time on the part of Government, or when sale has occurred, and the purchaser enters on new arrangements. By this Regulation the written lease rules were somewhat relaxed, and the parties were left to adopt their own forms; cesses, however, were still disallowed. Parganā rates, or rates paid for the same land elsewhere, were inculcated; enhancements were only to be made under special writing; and notice of ejectment was to be served by the month of *Jeth.*

So far, we see rights of occupancy implied or taken for granted, but no attempt whatever made to define or classify them by dividing them into the very distinct heads of (1) proprietary, and (2) non-proprietary tenants: pains were only taken specially to protect the parties indicated above, who are not locally known by the names there applied to them, and whom we acknowledge as subproprietors.

The next light thrown on the subject is by Elphinstone's "History of India," which shows that in 1818 eleven out of fourteen collectors of districts not permanently settled reported, in relation to permanent raīyats, that landlords were entitled to raise their rents and oust their tenants at pleasure. The exceptions were the collectors of Etawa, Sahārunpūr, and Bundēlcund, in the two former of which districts, strange to say, according to the published reports, settlement officers failed afterwards in finding occupancy rights. We must conclude from this historical information that all the collectors employed in the districts that had been ceded by Oudh, including Azimgarh and Gorakhpūr on the Faizabād border, were unanimous in opinion that rights of occupancy were unknown in 1818, for not one of the Oudh districts appears amongst the exceptions.

We next come to Regulation VII. of 1822, to the promulgation of which has been attributed the creation of cultivating rights. The objects of this Regulation are described among other things to include the "defining, settling, and recording the rights and obligations of various classes and persons possessing an interest in the land, or in the rent and produce thereof;" and the preamble further sets forth the objects of "ascertaining, settling, and recording the rights, interests, privileges, and properties of all persons and classes owning, occupying, managing, or cultivating the land." Section 9 then directs the "ascertaining and recording the fullest possible information in regard to landed tenures; the rights, interests, and privileges of the various classes of the agricultural community." For this purpose the formation of as accurate a record as possible of all local usages connected with land tenures is directed, embracing "as full as practicable a specification of all persons enjoying the possession and property of the soil, or vested with any heritable or transferable interest in the land, or the rents of it, care being taken to distinguish the different modes of possession and property, and the real nature and extent of the interests held:" and further, "a record shall likewise be formed of the rates per bīghā of each description of land or kind of produce demandable from the resident cultivators not claiming any transferable property in the soil, whether possessing the right of hereditary occupancy or not, and the respective shares of the Sadr malgūzār or other manager, and the cultivation under grain rents;" because it is to be hereby "understood and declared that all decisions on the demands of the zamīndārs shall hereafter be regulated by the rates of rent and mode of payment allowed and ascertained at the settlement, and recorded in the 'Collector's Proceedings,' until distinctly altered by mutual agreement, or after full investigation in a regular suit." Sections 14 and 16 gave the officer revising settlements power "to declare the nature and extent of interests possessed by persons occupying land," and also "authority to take cognisance of claims to the property and possession of land."

We have it on the authority of Mr Muir of the Sadr Board, who was employed in the North-Western Settlement, that "the rule enjoined at the settlement under IX of 1833 was to record in the *Khateoni*, every cultivating holding under the denomination of proprietary, hereditary, non-hereditary, or service, and to secure the complete classification of the area under these heads; the total of each class is required to be given in the English Statement No II. On referring to the statement in question, the record will be found to be (1) sīr of zamīndār, (2) cultivated by proprietors, (3) by hereditary cultivators, and (4) tenants-at-will, without any distinction between the two all-important classes of *proprietary* and *non-proprietary* cultivators; and I have searched in vain in the Board's "printed Circulars," and in the "Directions," for any detailed rules for the guidance of Settlement Officers in giving effect to the above laws (VII. of 1822, and IX. of 1833). The only orders on the subject are contained in paragraph 172, printed Circular No 1. This Circular bears date the 9th April 1859, but it would appear from the wording of the paragraph which I shall here quote, that it had previously been issued as an ordinary circular. "I am directed to request that you will impress on the Settlement Officers the necessity of having the settlement of liabilities and record of administration drawn out with every possible care. Some officers have so far misapprehended the Board's orders (not published) as to leave it entirely to the zamīndārs to furnish any rent-roll they choose, without any reference to the consent of the ryots. The consequence has been very injurious, and summary suits are filed, while the Collector is not in possession of the only document which ought to guide his decisions. When the rent-roll is given in, it should be proclaimed in the village for at least ten days for the information of the cultivators, and any objections disposed of before it is finally accepted. If the objections be not adjusted by mutual consent, they must be decided in the same manner as all other cases arising during settlement."

Looking over the Reports of the last North-west settlement, we find how these instructions were carried out. For our purpose it is only necessary to allude to the districts that were formerly connected with Oudh, and the result is briefly sketched below.

Gorakhpur.—Nine reports by Messrs Reade, Chester, and Timmins are published, and the last named of those officers alone alludes to the subject as follows. "The rights of cultivators have by no means been lost sight of;" it has been explained to the zamīndārs "that the rent-rolls which they now file will be held in force through the whole period of settlement; no claims hereafter for higher rates than those now filed will for a moment be listened to."

N.B.—There is no allusion to any attempt here at any sort of classification; all are apparently treated alike.

Barely.—Mr Conolly was unable to trace anything like right to permanent occupancy at a fixed rent on the part of the tenants. The Rājpūt communities enjoyed low rents, but transferable tenant rights were unknown, and the zamīndār was without restriction till Regulation VII. of 1822 was introduced, "beyond that imposed upon him by usage, common interest, and good feeling." Mr Conolly considered that, "according to the usage of the parganā," the cultivators were "tenants-at-will till they advanced claims to the contrary."

Marādabād.—Mr Money says the rights of tenants were very undefined before his settlement: there was no proof of succession; provision was made that if a recorded hereditary cultivator left sons capable of cultivating, they were to succeed.

N.B.—Here we have the hereditary or prescriptive principle, but no classification into ex-proprietary and non-proprietary.

Badāon.—Mr Sneade Brown endeavoured correctly to have recorded the rents demandable in future.

N.B.—Here all rent-payers appear to have been treated alike.

Azimgarh.—I take this district last in order because it most concerns us, and is the most difficult of disposal. Mr

Thomason's published Report is dated 10th December 1837, after he had been engaged four years in completing the settlement. He made his non-proprietary cultivators into three classes—(1) those having an hereditary and transferable right to hold their lands at fixed rates; (2) those who have a right of occupancy at a fixed rate for a time, for their lives, or their immediate successors' lives; (3) tenants-at-will.

It has been laid down in paragraph 124, "Directions to Settlement Officers," that it is of the utmost importance that the proprietary should be carefully separated from the non-proprietary cultivators, and the former confirmed in all privileges to which they are justly entitled; and as to the first of the three classes above given, we may here dismiss it with the remark that in Oudh we have not treated the people who come under it as non-proprietary cultivators at all, but have given them a *subproprietary* status. Neither does the third class require detailed consideration, because as mere tenants-at-will they have no rights anywhere; while, if by prescription they have acquired an occupancy right, as they often have in the older provinces, they have ceased to belong to this class, and have been merged into Class 2. In Mr Thomason's second class are (1) ex-proprietors, who have been sold up for default, but who still hold *sīr*; (2) the old ousted zamīndārs, who have long held possession of some land; and (3) resident or non-resident cultivators, who have long held the same fields at the same terms, into which, in fact, members of Class 3 have merged by reason of prescription. Of this second class the sold-up (under *baināma*), and the otherwise ousted (say by force) ex-zamīndārs, are often, in Oudh, to be found in possession of fields; and if they can show any connection between their present possession at beneficiary rates, and their lost proprietary rights, their position, under existing Oudh rules, would be guaranteed to them as *sub-proprietors* for ever: but if there has been a break between their former proprietary possession and their present occupancy at ordinary rates, then they would be treated just as those coming under position 3, that is resident or non-resident cultivators, who have long held the same fields on the same terms; and no ex-proprietary consideration at annexation being proved in their case, they would be left to make their own terms with the zamīndār. These are the people whose position is more particularly at issue.

The Azimgarh Report admits that the period of prescription which constitutes the right (under which the occupancy title has been conferred in the older provinces) had nowhere been settled, but it had been ruled that land held (? possession acquired) since cession might come within this class, and a shorter period might fairly be assigned—"probably the civil courts would recognise twelve years as sufficient;" and here we have the first suggestion of a fixed term for the prescription which is first broached in Sec. 14, Reg. VII. of 1822, but which only became law in Act X. of 1859.

In Azimgarh the following rule of practice was laid down, "the better to define and secure these rights," viz., "That the fair rate fixed at the time of settlement should be invariable during its duration, and that the extent of land thus held with the right of permanency should be clearly defined;" and the result is thus stated:—"In the two first classes, (1) bought out, and (2) otherwise ousted proprietors, the extent of their cultivation and rate of payment has been determined; and in the third, the land actually held, and the rent actually paid, recorded." This entire procedure was carried out by the village patwārī in the presence of the villagers; the result was publicly advertised, a time (ten days) for hearing objections fixed, and at the close of that time the question was finally disposed of by mutual consent, or by judicial award.

It will be seen that throughout all this summary of acts and orders but little is said of *custom.* Mr Conolly alludes to it, and also Mr E. Thornton, who declared that "the cultivators who are not zamīndārs are throughout the (Sahāranpur) District, to speak generally, simply tenants-at-will;" and "in the Mazafarpūr District, where many disputes were brought to an issue, the same gentleman stated, "By far the larger portion of these cultivators have proved to be tenants-at-will." These are, I think, the only officers who have spoken of custom, and they stated it to be identical with what it is found to be in Oudh in these days. The Azimgarh Report speaks not of custom, and it clearly shows that the detailed procedure of that district was that prescribed by Regulation VII. of 1822, and paragraph 172 of the Board's Circular No. 1 already quoted, which had, in fact, no reference whatever to previous custom. This assertion, rash though it may seem, I will now, without a shadow of doubt, satisfactorily demonstrate.

Some of the native officials, including three Kānūngos, who were engaged in the last Azimgarh Settlement, still live, and in communication with the Collector of that district, I have referred to these men, and have obtained much valuable information through them. Their recorded replies to my questions are given at the end of this paper. I have had the final settlement proceedings examined of 426 villages in Parganā Nizāmābād, and the result of the inquiry is as follows:—(1.) That in 156 of these 426 villages the cultivators themselves distinctly stated that they had no rights whatever; and out of the former number the Settlement Officer recorded in 147 villages that the cultivators did not know what rights really belonged to their position; while in the remaining 9 he secured for them permanency of occupancy so long as the rents were paid. (2.) That only in 16 villages were tenant rights actually claimed, and in all of these the rights were allowed by the presiding officer; in one instance on admission, in another after contest, and in all the rest, on failure of the landlord to appear. (3.) That in 7 villages no tenants came forward, and so no rights were judicially conferred on them; while in 184 villages the mention of tenant rights was omitted altogether. (4.) And lastly, in regard to non-resident cultivators, the procedure was so uncertain that in 17 villages no tenant rights were recognised, because all the cultivators were non-residents, while in 7 others they were treated in all respects like residents.

Of the 426 villages under reference 39 remain: in these, questions of right, it was found, were referred back to previous records which could not be traced; we thus have the result of the judicial proceedings in the whole of these villages. It will be seen that wherever the cultivators came forward, whether they themselves ignored having rights or not, whether the zamīndār contested this right or not, it was recorded in favour of the cultivators, without any reference to or attempt at the classification mentioned in the Azimgarh Report, and which, we are led to suppose, was carried out in every village. That it was not so carried out in any one of the 426 villages in question is quite apparent from the proceedings of these villages, all of which have come under examination; but the settlement procedure of that day carried intervention between the owner and cultivators to a point far beyond the result of the judicial inquiry; for the last act of the settlement, as already explained, was to call on the zamīndār to file his actual rent-roll, and this done, to placard it in the village for ten days. If any objections were raised, they were disposed of; if no objections were raised, then the advertised rents of the rent-roll were declared, in the words of many a Settlement Report, "secured and defined," for the period of settlement. The result of this operation applied as fully to the 184 villages, in the final proceedings of which no allusion whatever is made to tenant rights, and also to the 17 villages where no such rights were recorded, because all the cultivators were non-resident, as it did to the solitary village, where, after a judicial contest, the right of occupancy of the tenants was regularly decreed. This declaration, that the settlement rent-roll was binding for the currency of the settlement, had, in fact, the effect of stultifying altogether the former judicial proceedings of the settlement as regards tenant rights, by introducing a dead level of equality throughout, under which the ex-proprietary and non-proprietary tenant, the man who had held for ten lives, and the man who had held for ten months, alike had his occupancy "secured and determined."

Lest proof should be wanting in regard to the assertion made above, that in 156 villages the cultivators repudiated their rights, I beg to add translations of extracts from a couple of the final proceedings of the Settlement Officers, and to observe that similar extracts are to be found in the papers of every one of these villages.

No. I. Extract from final proceeding by John T. Reade, Esq., Deputy-Collector, dated 3d May 1825, *relating to Mauza Ekrām-pūr, Parganā Nizāmābād.*

Chapter V., regarding chhāpparband asāmīs. The asāmīs of this village have, in brief, recorded that they have no rights whatever: they pay rent for such land as they cultivate. These asāmīs assert no rights, but they are not aware of what rights properly belong to their position. The zamīndār, in accordance with the usage of the parganā, never ousts chhāpparband asāmīs from their old holdings so long as they pay their rents, *or very rarely so:* even when the zamīndār gives the land out for indigo-planting, he cannot oust the cultivators for this purpose without their consent.

Order.—The zamīndārs are in future to collect the rents from the asāmīs according to the rates (*darbandi*) referred to above.

No. II. Extract from final proceeding in Mauzas Jājūpūr and Chedhāri, Zilla Azimgarh, dated 18th December 1829.

Chapter III., clause 3:—"The cultivators are hereditary; they assert no rights in their lands or village, but they are so ignorant that they do not know what their rights consist of. Since Regulation VII. of 1822 was promulgated, many resident cultivators have complained of being dispossessed, and whenever it was found that they were not in arrears, they were redressed; therefore, it is not within the power of any zamīndār to oust any cultivator from either his land or house."

When I say that, in the limited inquiry that I have now made in the Azimgarh District, expressions such as the above occur in the proceedings of about 150 villages, all dated within the few years immediately following 1822, we surely have proof positive of the truth of Mr Conolly's remark already quoted, that there were no occupancy rights in the North-western Provinces prior to Regulation VII. of that year. I have asserted that the practice in the Azimgarh District, in regard to the classification of tenants, was widely different from the description of it contained in the Azimgarh Report. This assertion I will now prove by extracts from two final proceedings, and these will show that, however excellent may have been the intentions of the describer of the system of classification to which I refer, that system was by no means followed by those working immediately under that officer's own orders, any more than it was by any other of the numerous Settlement Officers of the North-western Provinces, most of whom confine themselves to stating generally that cultivating rights had been "defined and secured."

No. III. Extract from final proceeding by John Thornton, Esq., 1833, *relating to Mauza Khyrpūr, Parganā Nizāmābād.*

Chapter II. section 9, regarding the custom of *Batāi* (division of produce):—"This custom does not prevail. So long as the cultivators agree to pay the (cash) rent now decided, the zamīndārs will have no power of reverting to the batāi system, nor can they collect in excess of the rents now fixed."

Chapter IV., regarding the rights and customs of the ryots:— "(1.) Old chhāpparband asāmīs. It appears from the returns that there are seven houses of these in the village, six of ahīrs, and one of kohārs. Their rights are as follows:—Ever since they held, they have always paid their rent-instalments; and so long as they continue to do so, the zamīndār has no power to make any changes whatever. (2.) Pāekāsht asāmīs. There are eighteen non-residents; their customs and rents are just the same as the above."

No. IV. Extract from final proceeding by R. Montgomery,

Esq., Deputy-Collector, dated 14*th February* 1836, *in Mauza Khyrūd-dīn-pūr.*

"In view of guiding the future collections, the zamīndār is to file a rent-roll under his own and the patwārī's signatures, which will be placed with the record, and in accordance therewith, nor more nor less, shall the collections from the cultivators be made."

There is no attempt at classification here; there is no "registration in the paper of village rights of cultivators, whether possessing the right of hereditary occupancy or not," but all are alike called *kāshtkārs*, and all are alike left to be secured and defined by the issue of the placarded rent-roll. The village Khyrūd-dīn-pūr, which forms the subject of this last extract, is especially in point in connection with the Faizabād occupancy inquiry, for it pertained to an estate half of which went over to the British Government at the cession, while the other half remained in this district; and the inquiries which I have now prosecuted show clearly that occupancy rights existed in neither portion until VII. of 1822 became law.

Turning from Azimgarh to our other bordering district, Gorakhpūr, we see the tenant question treated thus.

No. V. Extract from final proceedings by C. Chester, Esq., Settlement Officer, relating to Mauza Dhaurera, dated 16*th October* 1838.

Chapter IV., the customs of the raīyats:—"From the records it is apparent that, though the usual proclamation was issued, no cultivators of this village have advanced claims, either as hereditary (maurūsi) or at fixed rates (mukarruri), nor have any objections been filed as to the rent-roll of 1246 Fasli. No special orders are therefore necessary."

Numerous proceedings in this district by Messrs Currie, Reade, Thornton, and Stainforth showed similar procedure. From this we can only infer that the rent-roll having been filed, and the usual notice issued, without any claims or objections being brought forward, *all rents*, according to the procedure of the period, were to be considered as amicably arranged, or in other words, "secured and defined," for the thirty years' term of settlement.

I have now shown how, by a system of enforced written leases, Government gave an appearance of fixity to tenant occupancy (XXV. of 1803): how, by special enactment, it reserved to itself the power of making cultivating rules (*ibid.*): how, for a long term of years after cession, occupancy rights were "taken for granted" (Mr Muir): how in 1818 most of the Collectors thought no such rights then existed (Elphinstone's "History"): how in 1822 a Register of all cultivators was ordered to be prepared: how in 1825 and following years the cultivators of the bordering district were still found stoutly denying the existence of any rights: how, under the Settlement of IX. of 1833, most officers treated all cultivators' rights alike, the rents of all being irrevocably fixed: and it only remains to be added that, having thus arbitrarily fixed the possession and rents of all cultivators alike for thirty years, before that period had expired, we introduced Act X. of 1859, the radical change and principle of which was that, where this possession of our own ordering had lasted for twelve years, "a full and absolute title of hereditary occupancy" had, in the words of Mr Muir, been "created." Right of occupancy is by some said to have been revived, and not created under our rule; that it was a former institution under native Governments, but it had faded away under tyranny and oppression. If this be true, the plant was one of unusually slow growth ; for I have shown that in the Azimgarh District, a quarter of a century even of our fostering Government had not yet made the majority of the cultivators aware of its existence.

In conclusion, we were referred by the Secretary of State to the former custom of the country to guide us in making these inquiries, and we were to record, if possible, such occupancy rights as had been found to exist when the settlement of the North-western Provinces was completed. I have faithfully endeavoured to give effect to these instructions, having devoted much care and time to the inquiry; and although I must confess that my private leanings are in favour of their being recognised where this is possible, I have come to the deliberate conviction that occupancy rights were alike unknown in the old and the new provinces, until the British Government long fostered, and eventually established them.

I wish to add that it has repeatedly been stated to me by tallukdārs who have land in both the old and the new territories, that, as a matter of fact, a minority only of the cultivators or of their descendants, who were recorded as in possession at the last North-western settlement, will be found in possession now, and that, do as we may, the proprietor always will, and always can get rid of his unpopular cultivators, by stopping their supplies of wood, water, grass, manure, &c., until they yield, and that rules on the subject are, therefore, of non-effect. I have not had time to test the truth or otherwise of this assertion, but if it is true, the argument is a strong one in favour of non-intervention.

The Report of Din Dyal Sing, Kānūngo of Parganā Nizāmābād, Zilla Azimgarh, who was employed throughout the settlement, and has been forty years in office.

To the best of my knowledge, cultivators were entirely without rights in the Azimgarh District when it was under the Nawāb's rule, and until the fifth settlement was undertaken by the British Government. At that settlement cultivators were at first divided into (1) old residents, (2) new residents, and (3) non-residents. The procedure then was for a native subordinate to go to the village and inquire as to the length of occupancy and rents paid by the tenants; and he then made over the result to a native superior. The latter recorded an opinion, and passed on the papers to the Settlement Officer for disposal. This of my knowledge was the procedure of Messrs Reade, Cumming, Reade (junior), and J. Thornton, and for some time of Mr Thomason also; but as the work of my parganā had been begun in 1231 Fasli, and Mr Thomason found it unfinished nine years after that, he changed the procedure as being too dilatory, and ruled that filing the rent-roll would be ample protection for the rents and possession of the cultivators. Up to that change of procedure the result of inquiries may be stated as follows :—(1.) *Residents over twelve years.* So long as these paid the rents entered in the settlement proceedings, they could not be ousted. (2.) *New residents,* no rights determined. (3.) *Non-residents.* If these had cultivated for twelve years, they were treated as old residents. But subsequently, whether rights had been disposed of as just stated or not, a clause was added to the final proceeding of every village, to the effect that zamīndārs were to collect their rents at the rates entered in the proceedings. Orders were then issued for patwārīs to file a rent-roll for every village under their own and the owner's signature, in accordance with which all future collections were to be made. These rent-rolls were made out in the Settlement Office; and after signature by the parties indicated, they were advertised in the village. When the period of notice had expired, they were assumed to be final and binding. No objections were raised to these rent-rolls, because they were made on the basis of the amīns' entries noted on the spot, and verified by a superior native officer. The result of this procedure was that the possession and rent of all cultivators was alike secured, and the zamīndār could not oust them; and no distinction thus remained between those cultivators who had previously been held to have rights, and those who had been found to have none. The names of the cultivators entered in the rent-roll at last settlement, or of their heirs, are entered in the papers annually given in by the patwārī, and this is the only record we have of mutations of names of cultivators; and there is thus room for suspicion that all the changes that occur are not duly recorded. It is to rectify this that the patwārī has to give to each cultivator an extract of so much of the rent-roll as relates to him. The respectable castes are shown consideration in rates to enable them to pay a servant, and the majority of high-caste cultivators enjoy the privilege. This consideration was formerly by favour of the owners only; but since the rent-rolls were advertised, it has become a right. I am not aware that the matter was regularly investigated, either when rights or rents were inquired into. High-caste men, who have commenced cultivating since the settlement, obtain the usual caste consideration. The question of rate depends on the contract made. I know of no instance of a man who began at ordinary rates being allowed consideration for caste at a future period.

The Report of Janki Parsād Kānūngo, Parganā Mahaul, Zilla Azimgarh, who was employed throughout the Fifth Settlement.

There was no such thing as tenant right until the Fifth Settlement, when it was defined and recognised. Orders were issued to the amīns to show the resident and non-resident cultivators as such; and when the No. II. Statements were drawn out, the residents were shown as hereditary, and the non-residents as non-hereditary. This was all the inquiry that was ever made on the subject. In many of the "Settlement Proceedings" entries will be found to the effect that no rights of hereditary occupancy have been claimed, but in most no allusion is made to such parties.

It was an order that patwārīs should file rent-rolls, under their own and the proprietor's signatures, to guide the future payments, no variation from which was to be allowed. When this was done, and the period for which the rent-roll was proclaimed had expired, it was considered final. As far as I know, objections were never raised. The procedure in my jurisdiction was different from Nizāmabād. Rent-rolls were not, with us, entered in the field Register, and so our rent-rolls could not be confirmed by comparison therewith. Although there was no entry in the final settlement proceeding setting forth that possession of cultivators will be upheld, still, in practice, the rent-roll has been held to be binding in regard to both rents and possession. The zamīndār had no power to oust cultivators; and if he did so, they were restored.

The original cultivators of the settlement rent-rolls, or their representatives, will still be found generally in possession: any alterations in this respect are shown in the patwārīs annual papers. But as there used to be no check, it is not improbable that great changes in possession and rent may have taken place without being recorded, and to obviate this hereafter, patwārīs have now to give an abstract of the rent-roll to every cultivator.

The ashrāf castes include Muhammadans. Favour shown by reason of caste is sometimes equal to an eighth of the rent. This favour was not formerly considered a matter of right; the low rents were entered in the advertised rent-rolls, but they were not distinctly defined as of that class in these documents. Many persons whose occupation is subsequent to the last settlement enjoy the same caste favour in rates. The majority of high-caste cultivators enjoy the favour with us.

CHAPTER IV.

ON THE TALLUKDARI TENURE OF UPPER INDIA; (FROM THE "CALCUTTA REVIEW" OF 1866.)

THE exigencies of the times seem to require that we should enter at some length into the revenue arrangements, past and present, which have been made by the British Government for the exclusion, or the maintenance, as the case might be, of the more influential class of landlords who are known in the west as feudal barons, and in the east as tallukdārs.

The word, correctly written, is Ta'allūka, and is said to be derived from the Arabic word *aluk*, a leech; and just as this animal remains suspended to the body to which it attaches itself, so the word *aluk* is used in the sense of hanging or adhering. Hence ta'allūka technically signifies relation, dependence, possession, &c. In this view the nomenclature of the Lower Provinces and of the old regulations is the more correct, where the ta'allūka is the smaller, the zamīndāri the larger, property. In Upper India the reverse is the case; the ta'allūka is the larger property, to which the smaller zamīndāris have become attached, or have adhered.

Returning now to the ordinary way of writing the word tallukdār, it is not evident when this term came into ordinary use. It is not to be found in the *Ayn-i-akbari*, and it might therefore be assumed that it was unknown to the revenue system of the great Akbar; but of this there is ample proof, that the title and tenure existed long before the British rule.

They are mentioned by Mr Thomason as having existed in A.D. 1677; we have seen them mentioned in a deed of the year 1642, under the seal of the Emperor Shahjehān; and they are, therefore, undoubtedly part and parcel of the inheritance which we at different times acquired from the various native dynasties which we replaced. Moreover, the title of Rāja and the tenure of rāj (which, though not exactly synonymous, are somewhat analogous to the terms tallukdār and talluka, the talluka possessing many of the essential features of the rāj) are as old as the Shastars, in which it is recorded of this tenure of rāj that the property descends intact to the next male heir on the primogeniture system. Rājas and tallukdārs, therefore, having existed long before our rule, they were a part of the system which we took over from our predecessors; and as it has always been our professed system to carry on native revenue institutions as we found them, it would *primâ facie* appear that these men were as much entitled to our consideration and protection as any others that we found to be connected with the soil.

Tallukas have appropriately been divided into two classes, the *pure* and the *impure*, and we shall now show how these had their origin. It is asserted that at a particular period of the world's history, possibly about the time of Abraham, Upper India was peopled by Rājpūts. At a subsequent period these people had to give way to other sects, Brahmans, Buddhists, &c., and then for a term of years they disappeared altogether, either sinking into social insignificance, and mingling with the aborigines, or migrating to other parts of Hindūstān, where their superiority was still recognised. But in process of time the Rājpūts again became powerful, and once more overwhelmed the then inhabitants by their incursions under different leaders; and in the middle of the twelfth century the Rājpūt kings, or Rājas of Kanauj, had full sway over these provinces. To these invasions of the Rājpūts Mr Thomason traces the foundation of the existing proprietary right in land. The descendants of each chief, he tells us, multiplied, till at length, in some instances, they displaced all other occupants of the land, or at least assumed all the proprietary privileges. The members, he adds, were numerous, and each territorial subdivision is marked by the prevalence of its own stock. These all trace their origin to a single person who first conquered the country.

Those whom we now call the *pure* tallukdārs are the chiefs descended from the leaders above referred to. They may be the legal successors in the direct line of the original settler, or they may be sprung from a junior branch raised to power by favour, ability, or the voice of the tribe; but of this there can be no doubt, that these feudal lords whom we found in possession are the hereditary chiefs of important tribes, whose position, in the eyes of the people, had become hallowed by the memories of an extreme and not inglorious antiquity. Whenever, then, we meet with a dominant clan of Rājpūts, with one or more acknowledged chiefs at its head, we may rest assured that these have one or more estates which had their origin in a *pure talluka.*

But instances will also be found, and these not of rare occurrence, where large properties have been formed at a more recent period through the influence of official position, or by favour of the ruling power. Such estates have been designated *impure* tallukas, and they are to be recognised by the general absence of clansmen, and by the traceability of the origin of the tenure. Even such tallukas as these, however, will also be found to be surrounded by the reverence due to the prescription of ages.

It was at the commencement of the present century that our Revenue Officers were first brought into contact with the tenures of which we now write, and we are fortunate in having the reports of Mr John Thornton, "a Revenue Officer of distinguished ability and discernment," to enlighten us as to what was done in a district where "the tallukdāri tenure" was known to "prevail to a large extent," under our former Revenue system.

At the commencement of our rule of the Aligarh District, in the year A.D. 1803, we there found established a large tribe of Jāts, whom Sir H. Elliot considered akin to Rājpūts, presided over by a chief, Rāja Bhagwant Sing of Mūrsan. This man was seventh in descent from one Makhan Sing, who had come and settled there about the year A.D. 1600, marrying into a local family. The third in descent from this Makhan Sing was one Nandrām, who ruled from A.D. 1658 to 1695, and who also held an office of importance under the native Government. But it was only in the reign of this man's grandson, Kosāl Sing, fifth in descent from Makhan Sing, that the property got finally consolidated. The said Kosāl died in A.D. 1749, and was succeeded by his son Phope Sing, who acquired, or assumed, the title of Rāja. His reign suffered many vicissitudes; but he eventually left to his son, Rāja Bhagwant Sing, in A.D. 1768, rather more land than he had inherited fifty years before. Five years after this man's death the district came under British sway.

The Rāja of the day was then permitted to engage for the revenue of his entire estate being recorded by the then Collector, who was "guided by the documents produced by the Rāja," as zamīndār of some portions of the parganā, tallukdār of other portions, and mustājir of others. After five years "an *istimrāri* lease was granted him for his own life, at a jama of Rs. 80,000 for the whole estate, exclusive of tallukas Sonk, and Madan, which were granted to him in jāegīr for good service performed in Lord Lake's campaign." It is not, however, very easy to divine what this could have meant, for *istimrāri* means perpetual, and yet a *life* tenure only is mentioned. During that life no claims by village occupants were listened to; but when the Rāja died, about the year A.D. 1824, such claims were freely taken up, and "all those who considered themselves to possess rights, as being descendants of those who were the original zamīndārs previous to the annexation of their respective villages to the parganā, as well as some who only rested their claims on long residence and management," were, according to Mr Thornton, "permitted to engage for their respective villages with the title of Mukaddims."* And, moreover, "as Government had directed that the possession of the Rāja should be restricted to the collection of a fixed sum from every village, those mehals *in which no claimant had come forward* were left in the hands of the mustājirs (farmers) of the preceding year, or committed to other individuals on the same tenure."

* The Mukaddim of the Old Provinces has been thus described. The village manager, subject to the zamīndār: his office is usually hereditary, and he is the responsible man in the village when the zamīndār or lessee does not live in it, making all arrangements, and enjoying certain perquisites. He is also known as *jeth-raīyat*, and in Bengal as *mandal*. In Oudh the Mukaddim has been judicially determined to be, so far as the lease of the village is concerned, a farmer without rights beyond those contained within the four corners of his contract. As foreman of the cultivators, his rights stand or fall with the rights of tenants.

So it would appear that, although, as Mr Thornton puts it, "the principle laid down by our own Government of maintaining any arrangement which was found in force at the time of the cession or conquest" was the rule which we *prescribed*, the rule that we followed on the death of the Rāja who held an *istimrāri* lease, and who had rendered great services to Lord Lake, was at once to deprive his son of entire possession, and to allow him "the title of Sadr Malguzār, together with fifteen per cent. as mālikāna on the jama payable by the village malguzārs." *

It will thus be seen that in 1824, twenty-one years after our rule had been introduced, we reduced the tallukdār to helplessness by transferring without inquiry, not only the

* How much more just was the rule contained in Sec. 12, Reg. II. of 1795, on our assuming charge of the province of Bānāras!

The Rāja having declined to consent to the restoration of the numerous class of village zamīndārs who had been dispossessed and reduced to the situation of cultivating raiyats by his ancestors, they were excluded from settlement, if they had been dispossessed before the introduction of our rule in July 1775. The Rāja afterwards withdrew his objection (see Regulation I. 1795); but "the rule followed in disposing of rights under Sec. 16, Reg. II. of 1795, was to confirm or admit those zamīndārs who were in the actual occupancy, or who had been known at any time to have possession since 1775, leaving those who might think themselves entitled to reinstatement under this rule to seek redress in the civil courts."

The fairness of this rule is obvious, for it left the onus of proving the right with the party out of possession; but in our subsequent procedure in the Mursan and other estates we actually dispossessed the tallukdār, and threw the onus on *him* of proving a right which he had exercised for generations.

The reason assigned for prohibiting the civil courts from taking cognisance of claims in cases of dispossession before July 1775, was that the "zamīndāri rights had been resumed by the preceding native Government, and not having in view the claims of individuals against each other." (See Cl. 3, sec. 25, Reg. XXII. of 1795, Harington's "Analysis," vol. ii., p. 280.)

possession of those villages which had been claimed by persons, who, in the words of Mr Thornton, "considered themselves to possess rights," but also all those villages in which no persons whatever came forward to claim under any such supposititious considerations.

Things went on after this manner until the settlement under Regulation VIII. of 1822 was effected, and this was entrusted to the able officer whom we have named. We cannot precisely say when he commenced operations on Talluka Mūrsan, but his completion report is dated December 1834, and supposing that the settlement of the estate took a year to be effected, it will follow that when Mr Thornton commenced his investigations and labours, the Rāja had been nearly ten years out of possession of his villages, that possession having been transferred by us in A.D. 1824 to the farmers, whether they were claimants of intermediate rights or not. It will be admitted, that after recognising the father as sole proprietor for twenty-one years, we adopted a strong measure in depriving the son, without inquiry, of possession: and having kept the latter for ten years out of that possession which we had in the meantime transferred to his opponents, we next proceeded to ascertain whether, in the case of each and every village in the estate, there existed two rights, a superior (the Rājas), and an inferior (the former zamīndārs), or whether there existed a single right only, that of the Rāja, as hereditary proprietor.

We may mention at this stage that, according to Mr Thornton, when Rāja Bhagwant Sing, who had the perpetual lease, died in the year 1824, the different villages which composed his estate were found to have been incorporated into that estate at different intervals, ranging from thirty to one hundred and forty years previously; and there is nothing in the report before us to show that the important element of *time* was at all taken into consideration in the procedure then adopted. The shortest period that any single village had been in the estate at the outset of British rule was nine, the longest one hundred and sixteen years; and yet no distinction seems to have been made, no discrimination exercised, but all were treated alike. It is true that in the year A.D. 1805 a law was passed that claims to set aside transfers carried out by force or fraud might be heard any time within sixty years; but there is nothing in the "Settlement Report" to show that force or fraud were ever urged in any of these cases, while transactions that are admitted to have held good for one hundred and forty years were, on the death of Rāja Bhagwant Sing in 1824, summarily set aside without inquiry.

Next, as to the search for the double right under Regulation VII. of 1822, to which we have alluded, and which, as we have shown, was made ten years after the Rāja was set aside, the intermediate holders having previously been twenty-one years, at the very least, out of possession. "After the fullest and most patient investigation, I have found that in about two-thirds of the parganā, the descendants of the original zamīndārs, who held the villages before they came under the Rāja's authority, are still forthcoming, and that neither by their own act, nor by the will of the former Government, have they forfeited their right of managing their respective estates as long as they shall pay the revenue demanded from them."

The estates of these men, it will be remembered, were absorbed, from nine to one hundred and sixteen years before our rule, and there is nothing in Mr Thornton's report to show that any one of them was in possession of the management of the village till he was restored by us, twenty-one years after our rule began.

Referring to the assertion that "neither by their own act, nor by the will of the former Government," had these persons forfeited the right of management, it is to be observed that Mr Thornton records that the Rāja raised the plea that the ancestors of these persons had sold that right to his father, "in return for his discharging some arrears of revenue due to the Government of the time;" but, he adds, "it appeared, on examination, that these transactions were rather between the amils and Bhagwant Sing than between the Rāja and the zamīndārs; or, at all events, that the inconsiderable number of the latter who were present at the time contemplated nothing more than the annexation of their villages to the parganā, and the consequent transfer of their future payments from the amil to the Rāja." *

* We cannot refrain from quoting here some passages from the writings of Mr H. St G. Tucker, who was repeatedly chairman of the Court of Directors:—

"The tallukdārs and zamīndārs of the Doāb are, I believe, the growth of ages; and both Jāts, Gūjars, and other Hindūs have been maintained in their possessions, although in the immediate neighbourhood of the principal seat of the Muhammadan Government.

"The tallukdārs and zamīndārs of the Western Provinces are recognised, by the Regulations of 1803 and 1805, as the parties with whom a settlement of the land-revenue shall be concluded. In setting aside the hereditary land-holders, we break through the usage of the country, disregard the claims of possession, depart from our engagements, and contravene laws which bear the sanction of the British Legislature.

"The way to conciliate them (the raīyats), or to improve their condition, is not, I think, by dissolving the connection between them and the inferior tallukdārs or village zamīndārs. The one we have, I fear,

In other words, this is saying neither more nor less than that every sale of land that has taken place in Upper India for arrears of revenue during our rule is invalid, because it was not done under the seal and sanction of the highest authority in the realm, since the order of an amil, or governor of a province, in a matter of the kind, is of non-effect. We may mention, however, *en passant*, that in more recent years our Government has taken a different view of the powers of amils

entirely displaced; but we cannot destroy the memory of their past, or the consciousness of their present, state. They were once prosperous, and they and their descendants must feel that they are no longer so. They are silent, because the natives of India are accustomed to endure and to submit to the will of their rulers; but if an enemy appear on our western frontier, or if an insurrection unhappily takes place, we shall find these tallukdārs, I apprehend, in the adverse ranks, and their raīyats and retainers ranged under the same standard."

(*N.B.*—How painfully true these prophetic words proved in the rebellion has already been publicly declared by Lord Canning, when he substituted the tallukdāri for the village settlement in Oudh; it only remains for the onward progress of the Russians to fulfil the remainder of the prophecy.)

"The tallukdārs and zamīndārs of the Doāb are not the mere creatures of imagination. We may call them *middlemen* and *contractors*, if we wish to degrade them by odious associations, but they are *the hereditary gentry of the country*.

"I do not argue in favour of the sudden creation of a landed aristocracy, but I would not destroy it where it is found to exist; and even where it does not exist, I would allow it to take root and spring up, as it naturally will do under the influence of laws which protect property and encourage industry.

"Some of the principal tallukdārs have been set aside and deprived of the management of their estates, and the great object seems to have been to introduce the system of revenue administration which obtains in the territory of Fort St George. I am satisfied that a zamīndār or tallukdār is a less objectionable *middleman* than a tehsīldār or amil. The one has an interest in protecting and assisting the peasant; the other seldom has any fellow-feeling with him. The raīyat can complain against the zamīndār; against the tehsīldār he dare not."

of the former native dynasties, and has, in fact, given to the grants and acts of such officials a very appreciable recognition.

It is quite evident, from Mr Thornton's report, that the parties of whom we write had been deprived of their right of management under the written orders of the superior officers of the native Government, at periods ranging from nine to one hundred and sixteen years before our rule, and that the Rāja had acquired these rights by the payment of a valuable consideration, viz., the balance of revenue due to Government. The most recent of these transactions was of thirty years' standing, before we interfered, in the year 1824, in behalf of those who had been all that long time out of possession of the right of management; and whereas we have the authority of Phillips for saying that "if an instrument of any kind is more than thirty years old, it may be admitted in evidence without any proof of its execution, such instrument being said to prove itself; provided it has been so acted on as to afford a reasonable presumption that it was honestly and fairly attained," it does not appear reasonable that these documents, which were not even refuted, and which had been "so acted on" for thirty years at the very least, should have been thus set summarily aside without inquiry.

The Mūrsan estate, when settled, consisted of over 300 villages. In one-third of these the Rāja was declared to be the sole zamīndār; and of the gross rental he was allowed to retain 12 per cent. for expenses of management, and 18 per cent. as *proprietary profit*, being 30 per cent. in all: the remaining 70 per cent. went to Government. In the other two-thirds, the Rāja was recorded as "hereditary tallukdār;" mukaddims (thenceforth called biswādārs) were allowed to remain in management, receiving 12 per cent. for expenses, and 3 per cent. as representing their right; the Rāja received 18 per cent.; and 38 per cent. of the rental being thus intercepted, the remaining 62 per cent. went to Government.

In the one class of villages, it will be seen that the Settlement Officer left the Rāja the management, *plus* 18 per cent. as "*proprietary profit;*" in the other class the Rāja lost the management, which was conferred on others, but retained the 18 per cent. "as in his own villages."

It is nowhere recorded by the Settlement Officer that he retained this as *proprietary profit*, nor is it distinctly set forth that he received it as *mālikāna*, *i.e.*, compensation for loss of management. Nor was a time especially fixed for the continuance of these arrangements, the duration of the settlement generally, viz., thirty years, being no doubt had in view by all concerned. It remained for future consideration whether the 18 per cent. given to the Rāja in those villages in which he was simply recorded as "*hereditary tallukdār*" was to be a *hereditary* proprietary allowance or not, and to the consideration of this subject we shall presently revert; but let us first briefly repeat, that the result of the Settlement Officer's proceedings was to leave the Rāja in possession of the management of one-third of his estate, and of 30 per cent. of the rental of that portion, and of 18 per cent. of the gross-rental of the other two-thirds, as mālikāna, *i.e.*, compensation for perpetual loss of management, and also for the loss of all share in any future enhancement that might accrue from good government, or other similar cause.

We have no means of knowing the precise orders that were passed on these proposals of the Settlement Officer, but we do know that Talluka Mūrsan became the leading case in the disposal of all other talluka settlements in the north-west; and we further know that they gave rise to differences of opinion and correspondence, to which we shall now allude.

In the year 1843 discussions arose amongst the members of the Sadr Board, Agra, on the subject of these tallukdāri tenures, and on the 17th January 1844, Mr Thomason issued his memorable instructions on the Board's reference. Having stated that conflicting opinions and procedure, and consequent uncertainty of title, had produced deterioration of property, the Lieutenant-Governor pointed out that tallukas were mahals of the nature contemplated in Sec. 10, cl. 1, Reg. VII. of 1822, where "several parties possess separate heritable and transferable properties in parcels of land, or in the produce or rent thereof, such properties consisting of interests of different kinds." He also pointed out "that the right of the tallukdār was supervenient" to the rights of the biswādārs, zamīndārs, or communities, and was "originally created by patent. But it has in many cases overborne and entirely obliterated the right of the subordinate proprietor." The question, he remarked, for disposal judicially (by the Settlement Officer), on its merits in each case, is whether a village is exclusively the property of the tallukdār, or whether other parties "possess in it heritable and transferable properties," independent of the will of the tallukdār.

Before proceeding further, we must here observe that the above summary of the Lieutenant-Governor's observations contains two statements, upon which the entire question hinges of the propriety, or otherwise, of his procedure in regard to this class of cases.

In the *first* place, in pure tallukas, held by the chiefs of clans, the rights of such chiefs did not "supervene." As shown by Mr Thomason himself, in the former Rājpūt incursions a great leader settled in a parganā or tappa, and drove out the aborigines (the Bhars, &c.), who, according to the same authority, have no rights of property now left. These tappa or parganā sub-divisions were, in those days, mostly jangal. This is established by the fact, that in one of the eminently tallukdāri districts of Upper India, situated near that in which Mr Thomason gained his experience, the area of which is nearly fifteen lak'hs of acres, the cultivated area, since Akbar's time, has increased about 175 per cent.; that is, it has nearly trebled. The ancestors of many of these tallukdārs replaced the sparse aborigines, filled the jangal, and their clansmen and followers peopled the waste. The descendants of these followers, who were, it will thus be seen, settled by the former chieftain, are the people whom our then policy accepted, first as farmers, next as biswādārs or ex-proprietors, and eventually as hereditary zamīndārs or proprietors, and whose rights are thus loosely affirmed to be older than those of the hereditary chiefs themselves. It was surely their rights, and not those of the said chiefs, which *supervened.*

In the *second* place, the Lieutenant-Governor fixes the point for judicial inquiry to be, whether other parties than the tallukdār "*possess* heritable and transferable properties;" and yet, three lines further on in the same despatch, occurs this sentence, "The full exercise of the proprietary right may have been in long *abeyance*, and the right only maintained in existence by certain recognised and very sufficient indications."

On reading these two quotations, the difficulty at once presents itself, how can it be possible to be in the *possession* of a heritable and transferable property, when the full exercise of the proprietary right had long been in *abeyance*.

The explanation of this, however, is simple. It is a well-established custom in Upper India, that when proprietary rights in a village are transferred, a field or two is left with the old proprietor, as part, implied or expressed, of the transaction, it may be at a low rent, or it may be for a time, or for ever rent-free, for his support. Such fields constituted what is called the dispossessed proprietor's *sīr*. The possession of this *sīr* was one of the "certain recognised and very sufficient indications" alluded to above, as maintaining the existence of proprietary right. Other similar *indications* were groves that had been planted, wells that had been dug, temples that had been built, by the ancestors of those whose rights had been kept alive by the existence of these antiquities. But there is a certain fallacy that underlies all this. There is nothing about these "indications" to show that the proprietary right had not been intermediately transferred, either by the legal act of the owner, or by the incontestable order of a competent authority: and, moreover, a lease-holder, a sub-proprietor, or a cultivator could dig a well, or plant a grove, or build a temple, just as easily as a proprietor could, and therefore to profess implicit belief in such relics as these, as indicating or establishing former proprietorship, is to avow a willingness to accept testimony of the most slender description.

Lastly, granting that *sīr* is only to be found in the possession of the former proprietors, and that there can therefore be no doubt, where this is found, as to former ownership, still the question of *transfer* is not answered by that fact. Moreover, the possession of *one thing* within the period of limitation, cannot keep alive a right to *another thing*, the possession of which has never been enjoyed within the said period. If the former zamīndārs were found to have long had possession of certain fields on favourable terms, they had a full and legal right to the continuance of these terms in perpetuity; but the bare fact of their having possession of these fields was no ground for transferring to them the right, which they had long lost, to manage the entire village, such right having most probably been transferred by voluntary sale, or by default, under official order. In our early settlements there is no doubt that many a man whose ancestor had only held a field or two for generations, obtained the whole village, because such fields happened to be recorded as *sīr*. It has frequently since been ruled, however, by the highest Civil Court in the land, that the possession of *sīr* will not keep alive the proprietary right to manage a village, where that special right has not been exercised within limitations; and these rulings of the Courts of Justice, based, no doubt, on Sec. 32, Reg. XXII. of 1795, are sufficiently condemnatory of the contrary procedure which obtained when the North-west Settlements were originally made.*

Apologising for this long digression, we return to the orders of 1844. The Lieutenant-Governor went on to explain that it was for the Settlement Officer and his superiors in the Revenue Department, to determine judicially whether the

* We can recall to memory a note by Mr J. Thornton, published in one of the earlier editions of the "Directions to Settlement Officers," but not to be found in the more recent version, in which it was said that though the village proprietors may have been reduced to a state not much better than raīyats, yet whatever privileges they may have enjoyed above such raīyats, may be considered as keeping alive the claim to be restored to their original condition.

double right in a village existed, or not; subject, however, to ultimate appeal to the Civil Courts; and that Government could not interfere after the commencement of the inquiry. Power was, however, it was added, reserved by law to Government, to determine and direct which of such parties (superior or inferior) shall be admitted to engage for the payment of the Government revenue, and with the disposal of this question the Civil Courts had no concern.

Talluka Mūrsan is then quoted, in which "many instances were found of the possession by several parties of these separate properties, and it has been determined by the highest authority that the subordinate proprietors should be admitted to engage for the payment of the Government revenue." The Lieutenant-Governor, therefore, resolved to adhere in future to that precedent.

He further remarked that in settlements that had already been forwarded, questions had "arisen regarding the nature of the provision made for securing the rights of the tallukdār;" and he went on to say that "a proportion of the net rent or profit arising out of the limitation of the Government demand has been allotted to him, but it has never been clearly or authoritatively decided, what is the nature of this allowance, on what tenure it is held, or to what contingencies it is exposed." The determination of the allowance, it was also observed, devolved on Government, and not on the Civil Courts.

The relative proportions allowed to the parties, as already detailed in Talluka Mūrsan, were then discussed; and the rule was laid down, that in those instances in which there are subproprietors, when the whole demand was realised, Government would pay over to the tallukdār 18 parts out of

80, or 22½ per cent., without deduction; when the whole demand was not realised, the tallukdār should receive 22½ out of every Rs. 100 that might be collected. *

We next come to paragraphs 31, 32, and 33 of the Despatch, which we may briefly designate "assumption," "deduction," and "reduction."

A distinction is thus *assumed*. "The law recognises in a zamīndār, tallukdār, or malguzār, not being an actual proprietor of the land, a certain title of management for which it is equitable that the Government should give him some allowance. It is also just that a rightful manager excluded by Government from management, should not be left dependent on the success of the system of management which the Government may follow," and from this it is *deduced*, that "the allowance to the tallukdār is of a compound nature, consisting of (1) a fixed minimum, claimable under all circumstances, and (2) a variable sum, claimable at a certain rate whenever the collections may admit of it. The former is the

* In paragraph 27, it is argued that if 10 per cent. was all that Government allowed to an *absolute* proprietor, it is unnecessary to give to a *part* proprietor so much as 22½ per cent. To this we would reply that 10 per cent. was fixed at a time when the proprietor only received an eleventh of the rental, Government taking all the rest: so that whether the proprietor was in, or out of management, he received alike about 10 per cent. It would have been equitable, therefore, when we afterwards left to the proprietor a larger proportion, viz., a third of the rental, if we had also increased the mālikāna of those whom we dispossessed, in the same proportion. (See preamble to Regulation II. of 1794).

Adam Smith considered "the tithe," which is but one-tenth of the produce, to be a "very great hindrance to improvement," and yet, Lord Cornwallis' permanent settlement which, as far as the interests of all concerned go, has proved a marvellous success, was formed on the principle of Government taking $\frac{10}{11}$ of the rental, the proprietors receiving $\frac{1}{11}$, or its equivalent, as mālikāna.

compensation for the mere *title* of *management;* the latter is the amount over and above his equitable right, which has been given him by Government as of grace during his life-time, and is open to revision at his death;" and *reducing* this doctrine to figures, it is thus put: "The present *hak talluk-dāri* being 22½ per cent., 10 of this must be considered as fixed mālikāna, and the remaining 12½ as variable and open to revision on demise of the incumbents," the following rule being prescribed:—

"Paragraph 37. The minimum amount of the total demand fixed at the time of settlement, should be considered an indefeasible right of the tallukdār and his heirs and assignees, so long as the settlement may last. On the death of each tallukdār, the arrangement under the orders of Government becomes liable to revision, and then the surplus above this amount may be disposed of at its pleasure."

The Despatch concludes by excluding the *Birt* tenures of Gorakhpūr from the operation of the rules, except under special orders.

We must now beg the reader to compare these assumptions, deductions, and reductions, with the intent and purport of the able and intelligent Settlement Officer in the case of Talluka Mūrsan, which we have summarised some pages back.

The first Rāja under us had a lease which was styled *istimrāri*, or perpetual, but it was also said to be *for life,* and so not perpetual; the next Rāja obtained the settlement of a third of his property as hereditary zamīndār, and he was "recorded" as "hereditary tallukdār" of the other two-thirds. In the former portion he got, besides other things, 18 per cent. as "*proprietary profit;*" and in the latter he also got 18 per cent., "as in *his own villages*," as proprietary profit. The settlement was for thirty years, but there is no mention made as to whether the terms just detailed were for that period, for the lifetime of the then Rāja, or for ever. The inference is, that the executive part of the arrangement was to hold good for the thirty years' term of settlement, and the judicial part, for ever. But it will be seen from the Despatch we have quoted, that the arrangements made, and apparently approved in 1834, were subsequently ruled to be for the life of the incumbent only, after which the mālikāna allowance might be reduced, and was reduced, to the minimum of 10 per cent. !

The Despatch, from which we have so largely quoted, was laid before the Supreme Government with a very able explanatory memorandum by the Lieutenant-Governor, dated the 31st January 1844. It is there elucidated that in Talluka Mūrsan the Settlement Officer proposed to take engagements from the tallukdār for the whole estate, and that the biswādārs should be secured by sub-leases.* The 18 per cent. of the rental proposed for the tallukdār was to cover the cost and risk of collection, as well as to represent his right to the estate. But the Board and Government disallowed the arrangement. They admitted the biswādārs to engage direct, and took upon themselves the cost and risk of collection; but they still gave the tallukdār the allowance of 18 per cent. upon the assumed rental, as a money payment from the Government Treasury, declaring this to be "a grant of favour. and not a claim of right,† to be open to revision on the

* A most proper proposal, and similar in effect to the system now being worked out in Oudh.

† Read with this the following remark by Mr H. St G. Tucker,

demise of the person to whom it was given." This course of proceeding, it was further added, received the sanction of the Honourable Court of Directors.

When the settlement of the North-west Provinces was nearly complete, the settlement of a talluka in Mynpūri, upon the above principles, was reported for sanction. This sanction, according to Mr Thomason, "the then Government * declined to give, and was disposed to admit the tallukdār to engagement in this instance; and evinced an evident desire to retrace its steps in all the other settlements of tallukas which had been made; the tallukdārs were considered injured persons, who were to be encouraged and assisted in their efforts to recover possession of property from which they had been wrongly excluded." But no final orders, in the above sense, had been passed. It was next admitted by the Lieutenant-Governor that there had been ambiguity in Talluka Mūrsan, which had been made the leading case; and it was also admitted that the question originally "was not one *of justice so much as of expediency*," but Mr Thomason determined to adhere to the established course of proceedings, and to settle all doubts by insisting on the following main points:—

Firstly, In settlements yet remaining for orders it has been determined to admit the biswādārs to engagements, and give the tallukdār his allowance from the Government Treasury.

ex-Chairman of the Court of Directors:—"I maintain that there are parties in the Ceded and Conquered Provinces, possessing a beneficial interest in the land, whose rights are susceptible of much more direct proof than those arbitrarily assigned to the raīyat, and who cannot be reduced to the condition of mere pensioners without signal injustice."

* That of Mr J. C. Robertson.

Secondly, The nature and incidents of the tallukdār's allowance have been fixed. It has been determined to be a percentage on the Government collections, *i.e.*, 22½ out of every Rs. 100 collected, but with a provision that the total sum is never to fall below $\frac{1}{20}$ of the total demand of Government from the biswādāri villages at the time of settlement, such being the highest amount fixed by law * as compensation to be given to a proprietor who is not admitted to engage.

Thirdly, A course of proceeding has been laid down in all cases which can occur, whether of default of the biswādārs from over-assessment, or of sale or purchase of the rights of one or other of the parties, or of decisions by the Civil Courts affecting their rights.

The Lieutenant-Governor further pointed out that diffi-

* We consider it to have been a defect of our former administrators to refer all such questions as this to the *laws* which we had intermediately made, and that *custom* was by no means sufficiently studied by them. Mr Thomason is constantly found relying on law rather than on custom. This blame attaches to the Indian authorities only, and not to the Home Government, for when arrangements were being made for the permanent settlement of Bengal, the orders of the Court of Directors were as follows :—"As preparatory to it (the settlement) we direct that you ascertain, as correctly as the nature of the subject will admit, what are the real jurisdictions, rights, and privileges of zamīndārs, tallukdārs, and jāegīrdārs, under the constitution and customs of the Muhammadan and Hindū Governments, and what were the tributes, rents, and services which they were bound to render or perform to the sovereign power, and, in like manner, those from the tallukdārs to their immediate liege lord the zamīndār. The establishment and settling the "tributes, rents, and services" of the above parties, was one of the principal objects of the 39th Section of Act 24, Geo. III., cap. XXV., passed in 1784, and in giving effect to it the Court ordered the settlement to be made with the landlords, and tha rules should be framed for "maintaining the rights of all descriptions of persons under the established usages of the country."—See Hardington's "Analysis," vol. ii., p. 174.

culties might arise, if the decisions of the Revenue Officers were contested in the Courts of Justice, which "have no definite grounds for their decisions, and are able to take only a partial view of the merits of the case presented to them," and he mentioned that, as a matter of fact, the tallukdār of Mūrsan had already brought suits, and had "obtained decisions which set aside the biswādārs that we had set up." But he hoped to remove these difficulties by examining the cases, and, if necessary, bringing them to the notice of the Sadr Court;* or if that was insufficient, a future opportunity would be taken of bringing the subject before the legislature.†

The Lieutenant-Governor, in paragraph 43 of his address, also observed that the result might perhaps be calculated to "*cause injustice*" (to the biswādārs is presumed to be understood), but as it was stated in paragraph 30 that the settlement with the biswādārs "was not one of *justice* so much as of expediency," it is not apparent that much good could result from the threatened examination of the proceedings, since the Courts of Justice could keep *justice* alone, and not expediency, in view. The fact is, the Government, in this instance, placed itself on the horns of a dilemma. The able and intelligent Settlement Officer had found a hereditary zamīndāri title in some instances, and a hereditary tallukdāri title in others, and had recorded them with a certain fixed money allowance attached to the latter title; he also recommended maintenance of the Rāja's position as manager; the

* See above, where it is said that Government cannot beneficially interfere after arrangements have been completed.

† Instances are not unknown of the Government having gone so far as to lend the biswādārs money to oppose the tallukdārs. — See Thomason's "Despatches," vol. i., p. 365.

Government, on the other hand, set all this aside, and put its own interpretation on the law.

The Civil Courts intervened and materially modified the results which the Revenue Authorities had brought about, and the element of discord having about the same time insinuated itself into the Board of Revenue, an appeal to the Supreme Government, with the Legislative Council as an effective reserve, became politically necessary. We are not aware of the nature of the reply that the Supreme Government gave to this appeal; but we find the Lieutenant-Governor once more urging the question on the attention of the Government of India, on the 30th March 1847. He pointed out the inconvenience that had resulted from the long period of limitation, *viz.*, twelve years, allowed by law, within which the judicial* awards of the Settlement Courts could be contested in the Courts of Justice, which latter "are not bound by any of the instructions from the Government which influenced the proceedings in the Revenue Department," the highest judicial court having "even declared that they cannot make themselves acquainted with the tenor of those instructions, unless they are formally brought before them by the parties." He further pointed out in regard to Talluka Mursān that the settlement proceedings, with few exceptions, had remained undisturbed until the twelve years' limitation was about to expire, when suddenly the tallukdār had brought no less than fifty or sixty regular suits in the Civil Court, to reverse the summary awards of the Revenue Authorities. He mentioned that such proceedings had a tendency to cast doubt on all such tenures. He expressed an opinion that when a thing had once been judicially determined, it was

* Query, *summary?*

unnecessary and inexpedient to leave it open to further legislation: and he observed that even as the summary awards for *rent* of the Revenue authorities could be contested in the Civil Court for one year and no longer, so ought the same period to be fixed, within which to contest the like awards for *titles* in land; and he therefore submitted a draft bill to that effect for the consideration of the legislature. The bill became law in the following year, as Act XIII. of 1848, with this modification, that the period of *three* years was fixed within which such awards might be contested. Nearly seven years afterwards, *i.e.*, on the 13th of August 1851, the Court of Directors (the same body who are reported, as we have already said, to have sanctioned the proceedings taken in Talluka Mūrsan) wrote as follows:—"Another question is, what will be the position at the next settlement of the tallukdārs who *waived* the question of their right to engagements, and received a mālikāna generally of 18 per cent. on the jama for the life of the first incumbent, to be, except in peculiar cases, prospectively reduced and finally fixed at 10 per cent. We desire to be more fully informed respecting the nature, extent, and duration of the *agreement* with these tallukdārs, and whether the *arrangement* with them was made for the term of settlement, or whether it was intended to be permanent."

Now here is a new light thrown upon this difficult subject! What could possibly make the Honourable Court suppose that the tallukdārs *waived* anything? For have we not just shown that the Settlement Officer, the Revenue Board, the Lieutenant-Governor of the North-west Provinces, to the contrary notwithstanding, the tallukdār of Mūrsan not only did not *waive* his rights, but he deliberately went into the Courts of Justice, and in many instances *gained* his rights, against the tremendous array of official influence that was paraded before him? And as to any "agreement" with tallukdārs, how could there be an *agreement*, when the Lieutenant-Governor, as we have already quoted, distinctly recorded that the mālikāna was "*a grant of favour and not a claim of right?*"

The Lieutenant-Governor replied briefly to the despatch of the Court of Directors on the 24th October 1851. All that has already been recorded above was recapitulated. He admitted that Messrs Boulderson* and Robinson, the then members of the Agra Board, expressed doubts as to the propriety of the course he had laid down, and that they advocated the right of the tallukdār or his heirs to the entire

* We may here note that Mr Boulderson afterwards published a remarkable pamphlet, denouncing in no measured terms the treatment of the tallukdārs when the North-west Provinces were being settled. The pamphlet is, in fact, a tremendous bill of indictment, and the proof is given of every charge in extracts from official papers. He actually uses the words "fabrication," "falsification of evidence," "misrepresentation," and he roundly charges the Board with such acts; nor did he spare the arguments of the head of the Government, which he denounced as "Jesuitical sophistries." He instanced the cases of several tallukdārs, and notably the estate of one in the Allahabad district, which consisted of 693 villages, two-thirds of which were taken from the tallukdār, a minor under the trusteeship of the Government Court of Wards, whose interests, the writer considered, were entirely neglected by the Revenue authorities, his then lawful guardians.

The pamphlet to which we allude was printed in London for private circulation in 1858, when the Oudh tallukdāri settlement was being much discussed, but it was a mere reprint of a memorandum of remonstrance which Mr Boulderson had submitted to the Government of the North-west Provinces, in his capacity of junior member of the Agra Board, on the issue, by that Government, of the instructions of January 1844, to which we have so largely referred. The receipt of the remonstrance was duly acknowledged, but nothing further was officially heard of it, and it never saw the light till the author, as we have said, reproduced it in 1858.

allowance of 22½ per cent. of the Government jama, for the entire period of settlement; but Mr Thomason could see nothing to shake his conviction of the justice and sound policy of his rules. He added that the tallukdārs never had advanced, nor could they advance, a legal claim to more than 10 per cent. on the Government demand, and he left it to the highest authority in the State to alienate for the remainder of the settlement, or in perpetuity, if it thought fit, the full allowance of 22½ per cent. on the Government revenue.

The reply of the Home Government to this despatch, Mr Thomason did not live to see; it reached the North-west Secretariat a few days after his death, and he was thus saved the pain and mortification of seeing his proposals negatived. The orders of the Court of Directors of the 2d August 1853, No. 13, may well be quoted here *in extenso.*

"Para. 1*st.*—We shall now give our opinion on the proceedings, in the course of which the Lieutenant-Governor, North-west Provinces, refers for our decision the question of the amount of hak tallukdāri to be permanently assigned to the successors of the tallukdārs, who *waived* * their claims to engage for the revenue at the settlement under Regulation IX. of 1833.

"2*d.*—We could not give an earlier reply to the Lieutenant-Governor's reference, in consequence of the absence of an essential document to which we have only recently obtained access—the original circular instructions under which the settlements were made. On this deficiency in the records we shall address you separately.

April 9, 1839. Jan. 3, 1840. Aug. 28, 1840. May 4, 1841.

"3*d.*—These instructions modified from time to time were printed in four parts under the dates marginally noted, and

* Again the Court use this strangely inappropriate word.

must be considered as embodying the views with which the settlement proceedings were conducted from the commencement.

"*4th.*—In the *Circular* No. 4, under the head of "Tallukdāris" (Sec. 24), we find the following passage:—

"Para. 175. The amount that should be allowed on a fairly assumed jamabandi, in proprietary villages under a tallukdār, has been fixed at 38 per cent., of which 20 should be allowed to the proprietary body, and 18 be assigned, in compensation for loss of management, to the tallukdār.

"*5th.*—These instructions were modified by the orders of the 17th January 1844, para. 30, as follows:—

"The Government and the tallukdār are entitled to share in the collections in the proportion of 62 to 18, or in other words, out of every hundred rupees collected, 22½ should be paid to the tallukdār. This seems fairly to accord with the nature of the arrangement and the expressions of the Board, as they were laid before Government, when sanction was given to the payment of the allowance. 32.—The allowance of the tallukdār is of a compound nature, consisting of a fixed minimum sum, claimable at a certain rate whenever the amount of the collections admits of it. The former is the compensation for the mere title of management mentioned in the Regulations; the latter is the amount over and above his equitable right which has been given during his lifetime, and is open to revision on his death. 33.—The arrangement was evidently intended by Government to be a liberal one, and this object will be fully attained if the minimum be fixed at the highest amount of mālikāna, claimable under Cl. 2, sec. 5, Reg. VII. of 1822, which is 10 per cent. on the total demand. In this case the present hak tallukdāri being 22½ per cent. on the Government demand from the biswādārs, 10 of this must be considered as fixed mālikāna, and the remaining 12½ as variable, and open to revision on the demise of the incumbent.

"6th.—It is stated in the Sadr Board's letter reporting the settlement of Mūrsan that the assessment was somewhat higher than it would have been without the hak. Government give up something, as without the Rāja's allowance a larger allowance might have been obtained; and the people give up something, as they engage on worse terms than other village proprietors where no tallukdār exists.*

"7th.—Whenever the 18 per cent. is mentioned, it is calculated on the *mahāsil* or *jamabandi*, as in the passage above cited from the instructions of 1841. But in the orders of January 1844, the hak is stated at 22½ per cent. on the jama (which is the equivalent of 18 per cent. on the mahāsil, the jama being the net payment by the malguzārs after deducting their 20 per cent.); and the proposed reduction is to be 10 per cent. on the jama, which would be 8 per cent. on the mahāsil.

"8th.—The question referred is, in fact, whether the orders of 1844 shall or shall not have a retrospective effect. The Lieutenant-Governor maintains that neither justice nor expediency requires the sacrifice of revenue which would be made by deciding in favour of the tallukdārs, and which he states at Rs. 85,000 per annum, for the time by which the term of settlement may exceed the life of the first tallukdārs.

* *N.B.*—No account is taken of what the tallukdār has been made to give up, viz., the exercise of the rights of property which he has been enjoying for perhaps a century.

"*9th.*—That the maintenance of public faith is more important than the acquisition of revenue the Lieutenant-Governor would fully admit, but he thinks that the public faith is not pledged in this matter. We differ from him with reluctance, but after the most deliberate consideration it appears to us that public faith does require implicit adherence to the terms in which the settlements were individually and in each instance confirmed. The case of Mūrsan in which reduction on the death of the Rāja was expressly provided for, may have been intended as a general precedent, but it was never declared to be so, and the principles of that settlement can only be applicable to Mūrsan, and to such estates as may have been settled with the same exception.

"*10th.*—All tallukdāri arrangements concluded before 1844 must be determined by reference to the specific arrangements made with the tallukdārs, as recorded in the proceedings of settlement, modified or finally ratified by the terms of confirmation. Whenever neither the settlement proceedings nor the terms of confirmation specify reduction on the demise of the first incumbent, the entire arrangements must be considered to have been concluded for the term of settlement.

"*11th.*—We feel ourselves, therefore, under the necessity of deciding, that when the reduction is not thus specified, the allowance shall remain fixed at 18 per cent. on the *mahāsil* for the term of settlement.

"*12th.*—It is to be presumed that the orders of 1844 will have been kept in view in all settlements of subsequent date, and that the settlement contracts will have been formed accordingly. In these cases those orders will of course be operative.

"*13th.*—After the term of settlement, the *hak* may, in pursuance of the instructions of 1844, and under Regulation

VII. of 1822, be fixed in perpetuity at ten per cent. on the jama or net demand of the Government, after deducting the twenty per cent. allowed to the malguzārs."

These were the final orders of the Home Government on this momentous question:—That they were a great improvement on those of January 1844 no one will deny; but it is none the less true that they did not go far enough. They appear to have been based on the idea that the tallukdārs had *waived* certain rights on certain conditions. Had the Government and the tallukdārs been parties negociating on equal terms, who had mutually effected a particular arrangement at settlement, the orders above quoted, directing that such arrangements were to be religiously followed, would have been unobjectionable. But such was not the case. The tallukdārs waived no rights; they were being deprived of rights long exercised, by our Government, and when they ventured to contest the summary awards of Settlement Officers in the Courts of Justice, they were threatened with special legislation, in view of their more complete suppression. What the Court of Directors ought to have done in 1853, was boldly to have restored the tallukdārs of Upper India to the position which they had long held, even under us; and failing this, the least they should have done was to grant *in perpetuity* the higher rate of mālikāna allowance, which, under the orders just quoted, they extended to the full period of the current settlement and no longer.

The Government of the North-west Provinces, in giving effect to the Court's orders, directed the Board to prepare lists of the cases in which the tallukdāri allowance had been reduced on the demise of tallukdārs without a warrant of a special condition for such reduction in the terms of settlement, in view to refund being made, and the Board were further to make it generally known that under the decision of the Honourable Court, the reduction in allowance would "take effect in all tallukdāri tenures after the expiration of the present settlement."

On the 23d December 1853, the Agra Board, in Circular D.D. followed up the above orders, by enjoining the preparation of district returns, and by directing that the orders be communicated to all tallukdārs. How these orders were carried out, we are unable to say, but on the 2d October 1860, the Agra Board called attention to the apparent difference in the rules for calculating revised tallukdāri allowances in paragraph 33 *et seq.*, of the Government Orders of the 17th January 1844,* and paragraph 113 of the "Directions

* We have already referred to Mr Boulderson's remonstrance against these orders; we cannot refrain from quoting his opinion here. "It is with the greatest regret I have perused the orders of Government of the 17th January 1844, on the subject of tallukdārs. Those orders, as it is my duty as a servant, I have issued, and shall do my best to fulfil; but it is also my duty as a servant to enter my protest against them, together with the reasons of the same; and it is also a duty I owe to myself and my own character, to state fully and freely that I am not and never can be held in any way a party to those proceedings, which, after the fullest and most careful weighing, appear to me condemnable altogether; and although I must needs use the same language in all private conversations whatever, I consider that confining myself to such declarations would be flinching from doing my whole duty, and that I am bound to place on record, in the openest manner, my condemnation of the proceeding, and to send the same to Government.

"2. I have repeatedly acknowledged the first principle involved in these cases, that it is highly probable the tallukdārs were not proprietors of all the estates they held; and that it was most just and most expedient to admit, in all cases where the rights of others were proved, and where those rights had been maintained and were found in existence, the parties possessing them, to settlement engagements with Government. I have repeatedly referred to the laws which give to Settlement Officers," and without apparently noticing the amendments introduced into the former order by the Court of Directors. In the Despatch which we have transcribed, they

this power of admission to the Revenue Authorities, and quoted them, time after time, to show that they restrict this power of admission to cases in which those rights had been maintained and were in existence. I have not seen the most trifling shadow of an argument against the validity and force of that reference to and quotation of law, not even an attempt at it.

"3. I have, time after time, protested against the operation of *a priori* arguments as to the rights of tallukdārs and the rights of others, as to what these must be, instead of what they are; which is the only point allowed to be in question by the law; and have repeatedly asserted, and with truth, and now again assert, that the proceedings in each particular case, I believe I may freely assert in no particular case of the many hundred estates which have been alienated from the tallukdārs under this so-called inquiry, have ever been perused or considered by the Board; that the proofs, therefore, on which the proceedings rest, have never been thought or made a point worthy of a moment's consideration; that the recommendations of the Board, therefore, for the confirmation of these settlements are to the last degree untrustworthy; and viewing the light under which they assume to have been given, are open to the charge of simulation and mere pretension.

"4. These protests have been in vain. The orders I am considering start with the admission, that these cases are 'judicial cases,' to be determined on the evidence adduced by either party; but proceed to say it would be better to treat of the general question first, and then to apply the principles arrived at to every particular case in succession. I had most earnestly deprecated this mode of proceeding, and urged (I am sorry to see how vainly) with the greatest force I could, that each case should be treated altogether separately on its own individual merits as a judicial question between individual parties, and not at all as a general question, which must needs lead to injustice.

"5. The effect of such a mode of viewing the subject is a breach of the actual stipulations made in each case by the Settlement Officers with the tallukdārs, and confirmed or modified by the Board and by Government, and the breach of these particular conditions is justified by reasoning upon what the Government and Board must have intended, instead of what is the plain meaning of the words used by them."

directed "that in case of revision on the death of incumbents, the tallukdāri allowances shall be calculated at ten per cent. on the new Government jama, that is, $\frac{1}{11}$ of the total payments of the biswadārs." In other words this was cancelling the order of the Court of Directors, and restoring Mr Thomason's abrogated order. Nay, more; for even Mr Thomason excluded all *birt* tenures from the operation of his orders, but under this vague and general instruction of the Board, these *birt* tenures have also been included, and whether the settlement had been made with the *biswadārs*, or ex-proprietors, throughout the provinces, or with the *birtdārs* or ex-*sub*-proprietors of the sub-Himalayan districts, the tallukdārs have suffered alike in either case. It has been elsewhere pointed out that these *birtdārs* were a creation of the tallukdārs themselves, and all that they had a legal right to was a recognised position *under* the tallukdār. Regulation VIII. of 1793 is conclusive as to this point. It lays down that only those proprietors are entitled to engage direct with Government who held their smaller estates before they were incorporated into the larger. Yet this clear law was set aside, and men whom the said larger proprietors had, so to speak, *made*, were given independent proprietary titles. These *birtdārs* are mentioned along with *gheruas*, or mortgagees, in Sec. 17, Reg. II. of 1795, as persons who were put in possession of their lands by the Rāja of the day, and as they were considered as having a permanent interest in their tenures, without any attempt to discriminate the precise nature of that interest, they were treated like hereditary zamīndārs—that is, sub-proprietors were at once converted into proprietors, to the displacement of the Rāja.

We have now portrayed some of the means that were formerly used to create and foster the local village system. We have shown in the case of a single talluka, which, strictly speaking, was neither a wholly pure nor a wholly impure one, but which belonged to the chief of an important quasi-Rājpūt tribe, how 200 out of 300 villages were taken from this ancient chief and given to the village occupants; and we have also shown that the estate in question formed the model for the disposal of all others similarly constituted throughout the Upper Provinces. We fully admit ourselves, that if we had a *tabula rasa* on which to operate, on economic grounds we should rather introduce a system of small than of large landed properties, but we also consider that it appears to us to be not only a point of honour and justice, but also of political wisdom, whether we be dealing with the natives of India or the natives of New Zealand, to respect the interests, such as they then are, of those whom we find to be in possession of the soil. It is too late now to retrace our steps in the North-west Provinces; it is not too late liberally to interpret the rule which has, perhaps, not yet been irremediably settled, as to the compensation given for the wrong that we have undoubtedly committed; nor is it too late to congratulate ourselves on the narrow escape we made in the settlement of Oudh, from following in such devious paths as those which we have just sketched. Our space will not permit of our further pursuing the subject; suffice it, in conclusion, to say that our reformed revenue system seeks to maintain things in Oudh as we found them; it seeks, so far as may be, to adjust rights as they have existed within the period of limitations, without attempting to revive those, the very tradition of which has been lost; it leaves for division between the proprietor and sub-proprietor a much larger proportion of the rental than was contemplated by the philosophy of the by-gone settlement age ; and finally, it seeks to impress upon the minds of the people the banefulness of an overstrained official intervention, hoping thereby to inspire in them the purer advantages of that self-government which the writings of Mr Thomason so truly inculcate, but which the revenue system, which he so earnestly believed in to the last, was certainly not well calculated to teach.

CHAPTER V.

A SYSTEM OF LAND-ASSESSMENT DESCRIBED, AS ACTUALLY CARRIED OUT BY THE WRITER, (AN OFFICIAL REPORT.)

THE revenue paid by the landowners of India is so closely connected with the tenures under which the land is held, that it may not be without interest to describe here the system adopted in the Faizabad district in assessing the land-revenue.

The plan adopted was to spare no pains in amending and confirming the previously collected and recorded statistics of the native surveyors employed, by close personal inquiry, and then to apply thereto the most approved tests, the data for which were always obtained from the people themselves; and finally to compare, geographically, the rate at which the assessment falls on a village, with the rates of those bordering upon it.

Personal inspection is a most essential point in making assessments. It is first useful in enabling the Settlement Officer to check the accumulated results of the labours of the various grades of natives employed upon the field-survey, which had been but recently carried out; and next in enabling him to observe points which are not readily ascertainable from records, as, for instance, whether the soil is gravelly, rugged, or level; and also, whether the means of irrigation are permanent or contingent. It is also required to enable him to ascertain for himself the average rent-rates; and where these rates are higher or lower than usual, to trace the cause. When the rates are low, is it from consideration towards clansmen, or the incompetence or neglect of the proprietor, or the prevalence of non-resident cultivators? When the rates are high, is it because the cultivators have subproprietary claims which they are struggling to keep alive, or that they derive perquisites of grass and wood from the neighbouring jungle, or that, amongst the agriculturalists, the well-known skilled and high-cultivating classes abound.

Another of the advantages of personal inspection is the facility it offers of forming a proper estimate of the relative producing capabilities of the well-known conventional soils. Personal intercourse with the proprietors further enables us to ascertain not only their personal condition, but the causes to which it is to be traced. If they are impoverished, is it by reason of waste, or recusancy of tenants, or is it to deceive the Settlement Officer, or from over-assessment? If they are prosperous, is this from light assessment, or large manorial dues, or from service or trade? The results of this poverty or prosperity are at once to be traced on the face of the village. On the one hand a numerous, happy, and well-clad community, with good new wells, and dairy cattle in abundance; on the other hand we have the reverse of this picture.

Personal inspection is more especially essential to enable the Settlement Officer to satisfy himself as to the amount of barren unassessable land, and of culturable waste. If there is much of the latter, is it required for the purposes of cattle-grazing and fire-wood, or is it from lack of agriculturists? All these points having been ascertained, the results are noted in a rough field-book and map.

In looking at a village, in view to assessment, it is convenient to divide the subject into, *first*, matters connected with the *lands*, as for instance, the soils, means of irrigation, and the crops ; and *second*, matters connected with the *habitations*, as the number of population, houses, agriculturists, ploughs, and cattle.

Soils are divided into *first*, natural ; and *second*, artificial. The *natural* soils again are of three classes :—(1.) The *loams*, which do not retain moisture long, take much labour, manure and irrigation, and produce two crops annually of every variety. These are generally put in the highest class. (2.) The *clays*, which are hard when dry, slippery when wet, and seldom need manure. They retain moisture well and are productive ; but hard to till. (3.) The *sands*, which include the various degrees of arenaceous soils.

The *artificial* soils again are also of three kinds, in accordance with conventional usage and geographical position. The first or manured circle, includes the fields immediately around the homestead, which benefit largely from cattle-droppings and the backwardness in conservancy arrangements of the people. The second or intermediate circle, which gets manure carried to it when there is enough for the purpose ; and third, the outlying lands, which ordinarily go without manure, are dependent on rain for irrigation, and which consequently yield but one crop a year.

The first step taken was to sub-divide the jurisdiction under operation into various groups of villages called circles, these being selected on account of the supposed similarity of the soils, distance of water from the surface, and other similar physical features. Average rent-rates were then assumed for the artificial soils of each separate circle.

It is a generally accepted opinion that the problems, which all researches into assessment are required to prove, are, first, that it is *useful* to discover what is the average rental value of any aggregate of lands as a village, a circle, a pargana, or a tehsīl; second, that it is *imperative* to ascertain the capabilities of each village to be assessed. Certain important details must be kept always in view, to enable the Settlement Officer satisfactorily to work out these two problems; and these I now propose to notice.

Problem I. It must be remembered that the gross rental of a village is of two kinds :—(1) the rental actually received by the proprietor, which we may as well not trouble ourselves much about, as it is impossible to ascertain it correctly : and (2) the assumed rental, which is ascertained by the application of reason, and the best known tests and methods devised by the many eminent men in whose steps we now tread.

The assumed rental is also of two kinds :—(1) that which can be reckoned upon as safe and unhazardous, such as the receipt of rents from resident cultivators, and the proprietor's *sīr*, where the agricultural appliances are found to be in due proportion. Where these appliances are under that standard, the rentals will necessarily be less secure. (2) That which is hazardous and unreliable, as the rental derivable from non-resident cultivators.

Non-resident rentals again, are of two kinds :—(1) those paid by those who live in one village, but cultivate regularly *the same* fields in a neighbouring one, deriving therefrom an average crop equal to the capabilities of the soil: (2) those paid by non-residents whose chief cultivation is in their own village, but who supplement that by casually taking a field elsewhere, where they can get it, and who, bestowing little pains on its tillage, leave it to take care of itself, and derive consequently but a precarious return therefrom.

Problem II. The capabilities of a village may be classified as present and prospective. The *present* capabilities may be called, (1) those that are permanent, as, for instance, the natural soils, the irrigation from the owner's well, the resident cultivators, and the irrigation from tanks, more or less according to season: and (2) those that are contingent, such as getting water by favour, the cultivation of non-residents, and the crops grown. The *prospective* capabilities are (1) those that are *probable*, as waste to be reclaimed, improvements by sinking inexpensive wells where these last: and (2) those that are *doubtful*, as a depopulated village becoming populated, expensive irrigation works being made, &c.

In considering all these capabilities, it will of course be remembered that only those that are probable will enter into the Settlement Officer's calculations, and not those that are problematical.

I shall now proceed to explain how these theories were made practically available, in ascertaining the gross rental. I first obtained a very elaborate statement of average produce returns through the tallukdārs and tehsīldārs, in which the yield from natural and conventional soils, as well as from land irrigated from tanks and wells, was shown. I next adopted four tests or calculations in the hope of arriving at a fair estimate of the gross rental. Two of these are well-known to every practical native agriculturist here and elsewhere, as (1) the estimated rental according to the number of ploughs; and (2) according to the number of cultivators. Of the others, one (3) is obtained by applying the rent-rates supplied to me by a committee of tallukdārs, to the soils according to the

Amīn's record; while the last (4) is deduced from four kinds of soils, viz., manured, irrigated, unmanured, and unirrigated. I shall here endeavour to explain these four calculations as clearly as possible.

I.—*The gross rental obtained from ploughs.* From my own preliminary inquiries, confirmed by the report of a committee of experts, it has been fairly established that eight bīghās is the average amount of land that can be fairly tilled during the year, by a single plough, in this neighbourhood, and the gross rental of such eight bīghās, contingent on the description of the natural soil, will range from 18 to 25 Rs. From this plough estimate the gross rental of the village according to natural soils is obtained. It remains, however, to determine what the nature of this rental is, whether *safe*, by reason of ample means, or *not so safe*, from fewer appliances, or whether it is *hazardous*, but with good or with indifferent non-residents, as explained above; and this I determine by a further process which will be explained further on, when I deal, by way of illustration, with the details of Maaza Arzānīpūr.

II.—*The gross rental calculated on cultivators.* Having satisfied myself by careful inquiry that a resident cultivator ordinarily tills in a fairly average manner two bīghās and thirteen biswās of land in the year, I find that the quota of each such cultivator towards the gross rental of a village situated in the various circles, ranges from eight to nine Rs. From this estimate I receive great assistance in establishing what portion of the rental is of the kind that I have described as *safe*, and I am also enabled to ascertain correctly by it one of the principal capabilities of a village, but this will be made more apparent by illustration hereafter.

III.—*The gross rental obtained by the application of the*

average rent-rates of experts to the natural soils, as recorded by the native surveyors. Having first made my own inquiries as to the prevailing rent-rates, which I have tested in many ways, I have always called on landowners to supply me with what they consider the fair average rates of the circle, and I have made an estimate by spreading these rates over the different soils entered in the field registers. I consider it a wholesome rule to carry the landowners with me in assessment operations, as in everything else. It pleases them to be consulted, and to have an opportunity of offering their opinions, and it makes them all the more ready to enter on their revenue engagements. Of course some people will say that these good men will take care to tax themselves very lightly, but I do not by any means bind myself to accept their figures. I use their estimate in corroboration of my own results and inquiries, and I generally find that the Government demand according to this test is about twenty per cent. under what the village can bear, or in other words, that the experts assess eighty rupees, where I put on a hundred; but as this is well understood by me, being forewarned, I am forearmed. After all, twenty per cent. is not a very great amount of consideration for people to show towards themselves, so to speak, in assessing their own estates. Are our own Income Tax assessments at home any nearer the truth?

IV. *The Government demand deduced from cultivation assumed to be* (1) *manured,* (2) *irrigated,* (3) *unmanured, and* (4) *unirrigated.* The ordinary rule with all native surveyors is to record as manured the fields encircling the homestead, and as irrigated the fields watered during the season of measurement. The results obtained from these entries, I consider unsafe as a basis of assessment, because no two people are of the same mind as to where the manured circle of land ends; and also because in this district, irrigation is mainly dependent upon surface water, the supply of which is never the same in any two seasons, and is therefore always precarious. I may give instances of the result of blindly following the above rule in the case of manured land. The homestead of village A is surrounded by brushwood, and for this reason the native surveyor entered no manured land whatever; while in village B the manure entry was absurdly small, because on three sides of the habitations the ground was broken and barren. In a third instance, in which there were only two houses in a hamlet, the surveyor entered an amount of manured land which was preposterous in extent.

Manure and water are the thews and sinews of indigenous agriculture, and as a natural consequence the portion of land to which they are applied is the backbone of our revenue system. Supposing a man to obtain a tract of waste for farming purposes, he at once looks about for the very best land to be found therein, as the future site of his homestead, and there he sinks his well or excavates his pond. To the uninitiated mind it may seem strange that any thoughtful farmer should build upon his *best* land, when he may have *bad* available, equally suited for the purpose: but there is sound practical sense at the bottom of this. Manure is so scarce that only the best lands can be treated with it, and it is confined to such simple material as ashes, and what is produced by the people and their cattle. Carting manure is nearly unknown, for there is only one cart to every twenty-two villages; so manure that is conveyed is laboriously carried by the people on their own heads. It follows that in this way only the fields adjacent to the homestead are manured, and hence it is that the township is built where the best natural soils predominate. I asked a landowner the other day why lime was not used as manure, and his characteristic reply was, "We have difficulty enough in getting a sufficiency of that to mix with our tobacco."

There is, however, one other way of manuring land, and that is by folding cattle upon it, and this is a method which can of course be applied to the distant lands, as well as to those that are close to the village. When we see a field of sugar-cane far from the homestead we may be sure that water is near, and that it has been manured after this fashion by penning cattle. In native estimation such a field would not be assessed as manured land, because the additional yield will do little more than compensate the owners for folding their cattle upon it. These are paid at different rates, and the process is chiefly carried on during the rainy season. There is not much of it in Faizabad, which is not a grazing district. Two *sīrs* of barley, a fourth of a *sīr* of molasses, and two pice weight of tobacco, is the ordinary charge for the use of a hundred sheep or goats for one night, and it takes them four nights to prepare a bīghā of land in an average manner.

In any moderately populated and healthy part of Oudh, a well has only to be sunk, and this is no sooner done than cultivators will flock around it as bees encircle the hive. The intrinsic value, if I may so call it, of a well, and more especially of brackish water, over surface water is keenly appreciated by all practical native agriculturists here : for this reason sugar-cane and garden crops are irrigated where it is possible from wells only, even where the expense of drawing water from a deep well is four-fold that of shovelling it out of a hollow on the earth's surface.

These observations clearly show the great necessity the Settlement Officer is under of looking most carefully to his manure and irrigation entries, and it was with a view of checking these that I sought for a method of testing them, so as to produce a more satisfactory result than the native Surveyors had placed at my disposal. By a prolonged investigation, in which I was greatly aided by several of the more intelligent landowners, it was ascertained that an average house with its inhabitants, furnished sufficient manure in the year for $\frac{12}{20}$ths of a bīghā of land, while each plough, with the average number of cattle belonging to it, supplied enough manure, during the seven months of the year that the droppings are not used as fuel, for one bīghā and $\frac{12}{20}$ths of land. It was also ascertained in the same manner, that in this locality eighteen bīghās of land might safely be relied on, as an average area to be irrigated from each permanent pond or well.

These averages have been advisedly accepted as fair standards by which to *test*, locally, the native Surveyors' entries. The results derived from them are by no means blindly accepted as a perfectly faultless *basis* on which alone to found my assessment. There are no doubt some officials who cavil at even *checking* assessment data, by any system, however carefully prepared, which is based on averages; but it is obvious to remark that in these days adjustment by averages has become a science. The operations of life-assurance companies, and of sanitary commissions, may be quoted in proof of this assertion.

It is not possible to reduce the results of the other sorts of manuring, as by penning sheep, scraping rich soil from tanks when dry, the litter of pigs, &c., to rule, as we have done with the house and plough manure. Nor can we take similar account of the water obtained by favour, or of the extra irrigation facilities by reason of great area of jhīls and swamps: but we avail ourselves of these additional means, in judging of the rental value of a village by personal inspection and inquiry.

I have now briefly described the four calculations to which I mainly look to guide me in arriving at the correct gross rental: and again, to enable me to weigh accurately the results thus obtained, I have further adopted a system of village classification from which I derive assistance in assigning the proper revenue rate which each village is capable of paying. This classification is based on individual inquiry and inspection of capabilities, and the results have been satisfactorily tested, by elaborate calculations made from produce returns. There are exceptionally good or especially bad villages, which will of course be better or worse than the average of class one, or three, as the case may be; and it must be understood that every village is not thrust absolutely into any class; but in weighing the capabilities of a village which I find is equal to paying a rate below the first and above the second class average, I note that this village stands between those two classes.

We have now gone over all the principles that have been kept in mind, to enable us to ascertain the gross rental of problem one, and the capabilities of problem two; the uniform application to every village of the result of this mass of information and principles so as to produce at once an equitable, buoyant, homogeneous and popular Government demand, was no easy task. This task was, however, facilitated by the preparation of two statements, which I call forms A and B, in the first of which all the Surveyor's and deduced data are carefully entered, while in the second, which is arranged geographically, with reference to the relative position of villages on the ground, are included the results of the local inquiries of myself and Assistants, with the reasons which have influenced the fixing of the proposed demand. I append copies of these statements, giving the entries relating to Maaza Arzānīpūr, which is the illustration to which I have already referred; and in case that form A, with its fifty columns, may be considered needlessly elaborate, I may mention that in the Central Provinces where there are fewer sub-divisions of soils and irrigation, the "General Statement," which is drawn out for every village, has just as many columns again as this form A. I will now add some observations on these returns.

Columns one to thirty-six, and also forty-one and forty-two, but excluding number thirty-three, contain the result of the Surveyor's labours alone as abstracted from his field-register, while the excepted column contains assumed data only, quite disconnected with the Surveyor's record. Columns thirty-seven to forty show the result of assumed data calculated upon the number of houses, ploughs, and wells entered by the Surveyor. Numbers forty-three to fifty relate to the demand shown in various ways. Some explanatory remarks are necessary for the elucidation of a few of these headings. To begin with number seventy-nine. In this are entered resident cultivators; and the gross rental, according to cultivators, is obtained by multiplying the number of residents by the number of rupees of assumed rental that each represents according to the circle standard: as, for instance, in the case of Mauza Arzānīpūr, which is entered in the statement, there are thirty-three resident cultivators, each yielding a quota equal to eight rupees towards the cultivator's gross rental, and this rental is therefore equal to Rs. 264, as shown in column forty-seven. The number of cultivators is an excellent criterion of the agricultural capabilities of a village. If there are not residents enough to take up the cultivation at the local standard of two bīghās and $\frac{13}{20}$ths per head, the inference is that the village is not highly cultivated. If the cultivators are in excess of the standard, then either they add to the value of their own village, by highly cultivating smaller holdings than the average standard just indicated, in which case we have a well-tilled village; or they go out as non-residents to adjoining villages, and in such case we have an averagely cultivated village; because each agriculturist can only till the two bīghās and $\frac{13}{20}$ths assigned to him, in an average manner. To refer once more to our illustration: in Arzānīpūr there are thirty-three resident cultivators, while forty-five are required to till the village even up to the average standard; the inference is, therefore, unavoidable that the village is not well cultivated. Column thirty is useful as throwing light on the subject of rent, and also on the quality of the cultivation: for where the skilled classes of cultivators abound, the rents are high and the tillage good, while the former are lower and the latter is inferior where the husbandmen are of the higher orders. Ahīrs come between the two sets in agricultural estimation.

Column thirty-one contains actually enumerated ploughs, and by these also we are aided in ascertaining the capabilities of a village: for, if the *enumerated* ploughs are only equal to the *required* ploughs, we know that we have a village the cultivation of which is average in quality; because one plough can cultivate eight bīghās, the local standard, in an average manner. But if the enumerated ploughs are more numerous, or fewer than the required ploughs, then we infer that we have a highly or a badly cultivated village, as the case may be. If there are few ploughs, and many cultivators, it may still happen that the capabilities of the village are good, by reason of manual labour taking the place of cattle; but where both ploughs and agriculturists are few, the inference is irresistible that the cultivation is *bad*. To refer once more to our illustration: we have four resident ploughs, while to cultivate the village in an average manner, fifteen are necessary. The inference here, of course, is that the village is not well cultivated.

A few extracts from my journal as to what can be done by a ploughman and a plough, may not be out of place. At the sowing season a pair of oxen begin ploughing long before daybreak, and go on till nine or ten o'clock. They begin again at three, and work on till after nightfall. A well-to-do cultivator has two pair of bullocks to one ploughman, and his plough will work all day. A two-bullock plough will, as already mentioned, cultivate eight bīghās, equal to five acres, in the two seasons into which the year is divided. A self-cultivating agriculturist will plough a rood and twenty poles in a day; a paid servant ten poles less. In preparing the land for the autumn, eight or ten ploughings are customary, but for the spring crop sixteen to twenty are necessary. In a week, a self-cultivator will plough two acres two roods, a paid servant will take a day more to do this. At this pace a self-cultivator will plough that quantity of land completely for the autumn crop in a month and nineteen days, a servant will take a week longer. In the same way, the former will require four months and thirteen days to plough his land nineteen times for the spring crop: the latter will do it in nineteen days more time. So that seven-and-a-half months are spent in preparing for the two crops, that is from June till November, and as opportunity offers, from January to June.

The entry about non-resident ploughs, in column thirty-two, enables me to find out whether the shortcomings of the village in the matter of resident cultivators, and resident ploughs, are compensated by the surplus supplies of these articles of adjoining villages: and as a result we find that our sample village is, in this manner, saved from agricultural ruin, by having the assistance of fifteen non-resident ploughs. I note here, that it is a matter for inquiry during inspection, what portion of the labour of these non-resident ploughs falls to the share of the village to which they belong, and what to that to which they are lent; and the quality of the cultivation of the latter will depend on the result of this inquiry.

Column thirty-three shows the number of assumed ploughs. By referring to column twenty-four, we find that the cultivated land of the village is 121 bīghās, and we know that one plough can take up only eight of these. It follows that it requires what I call *assumed* ploughs, to provide for the existing cultivation. The Surveyor's record shows the natural soil to be first class (loam), and according to our accepted standard, the gross rental per plough where the soil is of this class, is Rs. 24. If, therefore, we multiply fifteen ploughs by twenty-four rupees, we find the gross rental according to the plough estimate to be Rs. 300, as entered in column forty.

Columns thirty-four to thirty-six relate to irrigation, and

the reason for the details is to enable me to judge as to how much of the irrigation is permanent, precarious, or contingent. For instance, in this village, by both the Surveyor's record and the deduced estimate, there is an ample supply of water; but the details show at a glance that the supply is not *permanent*, because there are no masonry wells: it is *precarious*, because there are two temporary wells which may fall in any day: and it is *contingent*, because there are three small ponds, which are dependent upon the rains from heaven. Columns thirty-seven to thirty-nine relate to manured land. The entries in these columns are based upon the number of houses recorded by the Surveyor in column twenty-seven, and ploughs in thirty-one. In our illustration it will be found that the Surveyor's manured area is entered at thirty-six bīghās, while by the house and plough test it is shown to be eighteen bīghās, and personal inspection has satisfied me that the latter is the more reliable entry.

Column forty treats of deduced irrigation. The entry is based upon the number of wells and tanks recorded by the Surveyor, multiplied by eighteen bīghās of land, the local standard, as already explained. In the village under consideration, the Surveyor entered eighty-two bīghās of irrigated land, while the deduced data gives ninety bīghās—inquiry has shown the latter quantity to be trustworthy. In proportion to the cultivated area the extent of irrigated land is large, but it cannot, as already explained, be relied on as permanent; and therefore, as regards irrigation, the village is not entitled to be classed very highly.

I now turn to the seven columns of form A, devoted to showing the demand according to various computations. Four of these columns show the results of the four estimates which I use as checks, and which have already been explained in detail: the other three show—(1) the demand under the native rule, (2) the average of the two summary settlements, and (3) according to the village accountant's rent-roll. The *king's* demand is rarely discovered, and when found it is always worthless; firstly, because in those days it was either inordinately high, by reason of extortion, or unreasonably low, from bribery; and secondly, because the cultivation has increased at least fifty per cent. The *Summary Settlement* demand is quite as unreliable, from having been in the first instance based on unauthenticated village accounts, which it is well known were purposely falsified, and afterwards raised or lowered very much on the *ipse dixit* of the pargana officers. The *village rent-rolls* are, no doubt, more trustworthy in this district than in our older provinces, but I presume no one would venture to make these the main basis of his assessment. I have already said that we may as well not trouble ourselves much about the rental which the owner professes to realise, and that remark of course referred to these village accounts. It is simply out of the question to hope to get them correct, but still it is necessary to keep them in full view when judging of all the elements that enter into the Settlement Officer's calculations in fixing the Government demand: and therefore they are duly entered in my form A.

I have now fully detailed how this form is prepared, and I will next suppose that the village, the statistics of which have been filled in, is about to be assessed. I have form B before me, arranged as I have said, according to the geographical position of the villages: my field-book and map are also at hand. Having filled in the columns "number" and "name of village," with the average of the several estimated demands, as entered in form A, I next consider, with reference to the entire tabulated data, and my own local inspection, what the proper demand will be, and having found to my own satisfaction, which of the estimates seems to yield a result most in keeping with the capabilities, and having added what I consider proper on account of culturable waste still to be brought under the plough, and also on account of manorial dues, and having still further tested the result by applying thereto the standard class revenue rate, after weighing the whole mass of evidence sufficiently, I fill in the total of columns five to eleven, form B, in column twelve. The capabilities of the waste land are of course well considered—and as to manorial dues, but little account has been taken of them, so insignificant were they in extent. Mahowa trees are here exceptional, mangos are rarely sold, most of the lakes are annually drawn dry, to the destruction of fish, and there are only a few abandoned salt pans which have not been used during our rule.

I have shown above how the twelve columns of form B are filled up. It only remains to state briefly the grounds upon which the plough estimate was accepted, as yielding the appropriate class rate, in the village which has throughout been the subject of illustration, and these grounds will be found in detail under the column of "remarks," in form B Finally, these remarks having been entered, it only remains to record the "proposed demand," in the appropriate column.

I have but few observations to add. It is possible that on inspecting the results entered in columns forty-five and forty-seven, form A, the suspicion may arise that the results shown vary so much that the entries cannot act as a check on each other. But this objection is easily removed. The entry in column forty-five, viz., Rs. 360, is the gross rental of the ploughs of residents as well as non-residents; while the entry in the next column is the gross rental of the resident cultivators alone, the non-residents not being included: and the object of the different method of calculation is to enable me to separate the residents from the non-residents, for assessment purposes. Next, it may be said, that it is impossible to find an average area of irrigation from such conflicting sources as a masonry well, a temporary well, a lake and a pond: but nevertheless, I find from long practical experience that eighteen bīghās of land give a fair local standard, not indeed as a *basis* on which alone I could venture to assess the irrigated area, but as a safe *check* which I can apply to the Surveyor's recorded irrigation, leaving it to personal observation to discover and note, that in such and such a village the lakes are far above the accepted standard.

From a subsequent assessment report I quote the following, as worthy of attention. It is very usual with Settlement Officers to endeavour to assess upon rent-rolls only, corrected to the extent of their ability, and such may have been the original intention here, but the idea was soon abandoned for the reasons set forth in paragraph fifty of Mr Thomason's "Directions." It is impossible to assess solely upon rent-rolls. Corrected rent-rolls are one of the many points to be kept in view, but they are no more than that. The following are some of the difficulties that have presented themselves, and which led to the relinquishment of scrutinised rent-rolls as the chief guide in assessing. (1.) It often happens that a good deal of land is held at favoured rates by former proprietors as a part of the transaction under which they transferred their rights. In such case it is manifestly wrong that Government should be asked to accept the half of assets thus reduced under private agreement, and to be deprived of its dues by a transaction to which it was no party. (2.) Two villages adjoin, and are demarcated as one, because they belong to the same party. The owners and cultivators have their dwelling in one village, which the latter cultivate at high rates, and they also cultivate the other village at much lower rates, as non-residents. As between these two parties, the high rates of the one village make up for the low rates of the other, and so they go on contentedly for a time. The rent-roll of the one is high, of the other low. In process of time, from some contingency, the two villages become subdivided; and if the demand is apportioned according to the rent-roll, which it would be on the rent-roll principle of assessment, it is evident that the village with the high rates will be over, and the other with the low rates under, assessed: the Government demand on the former would thus be endangered. (3.) There are instances in which the cultivators pay very high rates for their arable land, under a direct understanding with the owner that they are to gather wood and grass from the village waste. In this case, if the assessment is made on the high rent-roll of the cultivated area, and an additional sum, as is the invariable rule, is added for the culturable waste, the proprietor would be at a great disadvantage, for Government has already taxed that waste by taking half the enhanced rents which the cultivators pay on their arable land, for the privilege of getting wood, grass, &c. (4.) Many rent-rolls have been inordinately run up by reason of subproprietary disputes: to assess upon these would be certain ruin. (5.) Many proprietors are in debt to their cultivators, and pay the interest in a reduction of rent; to assess upon the rent-roll here, would be to forego the just Government demand. (6.) It is customary to bring cultivators from a distance, and to make them advances to induce them to settle. These advances are frequently not repaid as such, but are squared in time by a small addition to the rent; to assess this addition would be to tax capital in the manner deprecated in paragraph 65 of the "Directions." (7.) It was very common for a landowner in the king's time, to have in view some particular land which was set aside, in lieu of wages of servants and retainers; the village accountant was duly instructed to enter the rental of that land at double or treble the proper amount, and at that nominal sum it was assigned as wages. In many instances these absurd entries have run on to date: and to assess upon the rent-rolls in such cases would be surely folly. (8.) There is no doubt that the village rent-rolls do not by any means represent the landowner's collections: and therefore to assess upon them rather than upon the otherwise ascertained capabilities, is to forego much revenue. (9.) In many instances, rent-rolls have been nominally run up by landlords, and *their friends* in the village have agreed to absurdly high entries, which were never of course to be acted on, in order that rent-suits might be brought against *their foes*, at neighbouring rates, which rates were those nominal ones just referred to. However much the landlord in this and others of the above cases might deserve punishment, rent-rolls so enhanced are not a safe basis for assessment purposes. (10.) Lastly, in subproprietary villages the rent-rolls have often been found exceptionally unreliable. Where the tallukdār has been able to influence the village accountant, the rental will usually be found over-stated; where the sub-proprietor has exercised that influence, they will be found under-stated. The larger the rental the more will the tallukdār obtain; the smaller the rental, the more will the sub-proprietor receive. To explain this in detail would occupy a volume, suffice it to say such rent-rolls are useless for assessment purposes.

I will conclude these remarks by a quotation from a report on the results of some of the assessments conducted by me.

From an extended personal knowledge of the relative capabilities of this district, and of those which surround it, whether they be in Oudh or the North-western Provinces, the merit is claimed for the assessments now reported of being as moderate as it was possible to make them, compatibly with an honest regard to the due interests of the State. In proof of this the following remarks are offered. (1.) The Government demand falls at the rate of Rs. 3.8 per cultivator. It is universally admitted here, that the gross produce per ordinary cultivator will be Rs. 20 per annum. Of this sum three-fifths, or Rs. 12, will be absorbed as the cultivator's own share, and the remaining two-fifths, or Rs. 8, will go to the proprietor as gross rental, this being the proportion in which the produce is very generally, though by no means invariably divided, between landlord and tenant. Of this latter amount at $51\frac{1}{4}$ per cent., Rs. 4.3 will be paid to Government as revenue and cesses; and Rs. 3.13 remain as the landlord's net profit. It follows that as the demand on each cultivator falls at Rs. 3.8, whereas it might have fallen at Rs. 4.3, the assessment, according to this mode of calculation, is light. (2.) There are twelve descriptions of produce usually grown in the district, and the average yield of the twelve per acre, is eight maunds and four sīrs. Apply this average yield to the cultivated area under report, and the total produce will be

15,20,985 maunds of grain; convert this into money in accordance with the accepted average price-current of a given term of years, and the result will be Rs. 19,47,660, of which sum Government, according to the proportion of distribution just indicated, is entitled to Rs. 3,93,901, against Rs. 3,70,722, the amount assessed on cultivation. The demand fixed according to this calculation is Rs. 23,179 below the fair half assets authorised by the rules. (3.) It has been well established that about 20 per cent. of the cultivation is under wheat, and that the gross produce thereof per acre, according to the price-current already mentioned, is Rs. 18.5. Suppose a village to contain a hundred acres of cultivation, twenty of which are under wheat, the gross produce of these latter acres, at that rate, will be Rs. 367. There remain eighty acres to be sown with the remaining eleven ordinary sorts of produce. It will be a most moderate computation if we assume that these eighty acres will yield half the value in produce given by the twenty wheat acres, or say an average of Rs. 9.2 all round, which is equal to a total of Rs. 732, giving the gross produce of the entire hundred cultivated acres as Rs. 1099. Of this, the gross rental at two-fifths, the proportion of distribution already alluded to, will be Rs. 440, and of the latter sum, the Government demand will be Rs. 225. By the application of the average local revenue rate for cultivation of Rs. 2.1.1 per acre, to the hundred acres under consideration, the Government demand would be Rs. 206, and so by the calculation just made, the revised demand on cultivation only will fall at Rs. 19 below the half assets allowed to be taken, leaving any waste land that there might be in addition, to the good in the account.

It has now only to be added that these are the principles

upon which the Faizabad assessments were completed. There are of course as many systems of assessment as there are Settlement Officers, and we do not presume to say that ours is better than the others, but such as it is, it has been faithfully described above; it has now withstood the trying test of several indifferent seasons, without any apparent signs of serious failure; and this, after all, is the greatest praise that can be claimed for any assessment.

FORM A.

No.	Name of Tahsildar or Zamindar	Name of Village	Total Area: Bighas	Total Area: Biswas	Deduction: Unculturable: Bighas	Biswas	Mâfi sanctioned by Government: Bighas	Biswas	Groves less than 10 per cent: Bighas	Biswas	Total: Bighas	Biswas	Unculturated: Fallow: Bighas	Biswas	Jungal: Bighas	Biswas	Groves more than 10 per cent: Bighas	Biswas	Total: Bighas	Biswas
1	2	3	4	5	6	7	8	9	10	11	12	13	14	15	16	17	18	19	20	21
1	Bhee Narain Singh	Aramjpúr	122	14	24	7	...	...	...	5	24	15	5	2	1	1	...	...	4	3
	Areas by	Khasra	96	...	...	...	...	...	...	15	...	...	...	...	...	...	...	...	4	...
		S. Survey	97	...	...	...	...	...	...	...	...	...	...	...	...	...	...	...	...	...

Conventional Name of Soil	Cultivated: Irrigated: Dorsa	Mutyar	Bhur	Unirrigated: Dorsa	Mutyar	Bhur	Total of these Soils: Dorsa	Mutyar	Bhur	Total	Total Malguzari: Bighas	Biswas	Total Cultivation assessed at Summary Settlement, where procurable
22	23	24	25	26	27	28	29	30	31	32	33	34	35
Goind	31.6	...	...	4.1	...	...	36.6	...	...	36.6	127	19	...
Majhar	29.4	...	...	24.10	0.8	...	54	0.8	...	54.8	...	...	...
Palo	20.16	...	...	10.6	...	...	31.2	...	...	31.2			
Total	82.5	...	...	39.3	0.8	...	121.8	0.8	...	121.16			
					Zamindar's Khasra [illegible]					122.0 / 76 / 79	83		

Population and Houses: Number of Houses	Number of Persons	Number of Cultivators, with General Rate of Rent per Cultivator	Prevailing Cultivating Tribe	Number of Ploughs: Actual: Resident	Non-resident	Estimated Number required to yield the Highest Jamas of Pargana Rate and Rate per Plough	Irrigated: Wells: Pukka	Kham	Tanks and Jhils	Goind and Irrigation, deduced at Pargana Standard: Goind: 12 Biswas per House	1 Bigha 12 Biswas per Plough	Total Land	Standard Average per Well and Tank 18 Bighas
36	37	38	39	40	41	42	43	44	45	46	47	48	49
29	50	33	Kewath.	4	15	15	...	2	2	12	6.8	18.8	90 Irrigation
...	...	Rs. 8		...	...	Rs. 18	...	...	...	...	...	at 2.2	at 1.6 Dry at 12

Rates: Name of Article	Estimated Value	Detail of Net Produce and of the Government Share according to: Ex-King's Demands	Average of both Summary Settlements	Bhao-Rent	Ploughs	Cultivators	Bhao-Rent as per Zamindar's Calculation	Deduced from Goind and Irrigation	Average of those 5 Jamas
50	51	52	53	54	55	56	57	58	59
...	...	...	...	Net Produce. 300	300	264	203	...	
			130	Government Share. 151	180	120	187	160	
			0 12 6	Rate per Bighá on Cultivation. 1 2 9	1 8 4	1 1 10	1 3 6	1 3 6	

FORM B.

No.	No. as per Form A.	Name of Mauzah	Average of 7 Jamas	The most reliable Jama and Rate per Bighá on Cultivation	Purti and Bagh over 10 per cent: Area and Rate, Purti at 4 Annas, Baghs at 8 Annas, Government Share	Equal to Rupees	Jangal: Area and Rate at 2 Annas per Bighá, Government Share	Equal to Rupees	Bagh: Articles and Total Amount	Government Share	Total of last 7 Columns	Proposed Jama
1	2	3	4	5	6	7	8	9	10	11	12	13
1	1	Aramjpúr	167	186 / 1 8 4	5.3	5.4	1.1	0 2 6	...	...	186	187 / 1 8 3

REMARKS, AND THE DEDUCED JAMA AT ASSUMED REVENUE RATES.

14

JAMA BY ASSUMED REVENUE RATES.

	Bg.	Bis.	Standard Rate.	Govt. Jama
				Rs. a. p.
Irrigated	90	2		
Deduct Goind	18	8	at 2-2-0	39 1 6
Remaining irrigated	71	15	at 1-6-0	98 9 0
Dry	31	28	at 0-12-0	23 15 0
Jangal, Purti, Bagh			Nil.	
			Total	161 9 6

First-Class Soil.—*Irrigation* ample, but not permanent, being dependent on kachcha wells and ponds. Cultivation partly dependent on zamindars. The condition of the owners not such as to give hope of much future improvement.—*Jamas.* The [illegible] Plough estimate yields Rupees 300, made up of rentals that are both cash (Rupees 264) and [illegible] (Rupees 36). The cultivator's estimate is Rupees 264 [illegible] rental, but means, i.e., resident ploughs deficient). The difference between 264 Rupees and 300 Rupees (plough estimate) shows that 36 Rupees of the gross rental is paid by non-residents. These two tests tally, and they are also in keeping with the capabilities of the village. The tahsildar's estimate yields 203 Rupees, and the result is, as usual, between a fifth and sixth under the proper demand, but this is well understood. The deduced rental falls below the plough and cultivator's estimates, because the manured land is small (from few houses and resident ploughs). But, as a set-off against this blemish, we have non-residents, whose capacity shews to be of the better of the two classes, cultivating the same fields permanently, and working them up to a high standard of excellence.—*Classification.* This is a village which the natural soils indicate to be of the first class, the means of irrigation of the second class, and the other capabilities of the third class. Weighing all these points, I consider the village to be of the middle class, the appropriate rate for which is obtained by accepting the plough rental, which will yield Government Jama of Rupees 185, plus a Rupee for culturable waste = 186 Rupees, which gives a second-class rate on cultivation of Rupees 1-8-4.

GLOSSARY.

For the convenience of English readers the following Indian terms which occur in this book have been freely, rather than technically, rendered.

A

Abwāb.—Cesses formerly collected in addition to revenue and rent, not now allowed.

Amānat.—Literally trust. Nazims managing on the part of Government, in contradistinction to those who contracted for the office, were said to hold amānat: the same term was used to signify that a village had been included in the rent-roll of a tallukdār as a measure of safety.

Amīn.—The native Surveyor, by whom the field survey was conducted.

Arzal.—All low-caste cultivators are so styled.

Asāmī.—A cultivator generally.

Ashrāf.—High-caste cultivators, such as Brahmins and Chatris.

B

Bāch'h.—The system by which pecuniary responsibility is

distributed amongst the members of a coparcenary community.

Baghāt.—Literally groves, the tenure relating thereto.

Baikitāt.—Literally purchased patches of land, held within the limits of a village by others than the owner of the latter.

Bai-nāma.—A deed of sale.

Barbasti.—A quit-rent on tenures formerly rent-free.

Bīghā.—A land measure, which varies in size in different places; the standard bīghā is five-eighths of an acre.

Birt.—A purchased or conferred subordinate land-improving tenure; the holder of it is called birtīa or birtdār.

Biswā.—The twentieth part of a bīghā.

Biswādārs.—The village occupants who were generally settled with to the exclusion of tallukdārs in our older provinces.

Biswī.—A form of petty mortgage, which is fully explained in the text; the holder is called biswīdār.

C

Chakbat.—A distribution of land in lumps or blocks, in contradistinction to khetbat, which is according to fields.

Chhapparband.—One of the names by which resident cultivators are mentioned in our old laws.

D

Darbandi.—Rent-rates are so styled.

Dīdāri.—An allowance in land or money received by old zamīndārs for support on selling their estate.

G

Gherūa.—A petty mortgage holder, mentioned in old laws.

I

Ijāra.—A farming lease.

Istimrār.—Perpetual; the holder at fixed rates was called istimrārdār.

J

Jægīr.—It locally means land held in lieu of wages, the holder being styled jægīrdār.

Jama.—The revenue paid to Government, also the rent of a leased village. The village rent-roll is called the jamabandī.

Jamōg.—The process of collecting revenue or rent by paid agent, to the exclusion of the proprietor or sub-proprietor, such agent being called the jamōgdār.

K

Kabūliyat.—The engagement to pay the Government revenue, the holder of which is called the kabūliyatdār.

Kabz.—The system under which the revenue of land was assigned by Government to some of its servants to be realised in lieu of their wages, such being styled kabzdār.

Kachcha.—When the cultivators pay direct to a landowner, or when the village occupants paid direct to the Officers of the native Government, the arrangement was known as holding kachcha or khām. A temporary, in contradistinction to a masonry well, is so designated.

Kachehri.—A court-house or office.

Kami-rakūmāt.—Unauthorised remissions of revenue, often winked at by the Officials of native Governments.

Kānūngo.—A Pargana Officer, and repository for general information. The superintendent of village accountants.

Kāshtkār.—A cultivator, see also Khudkasht and Asāmī.

Khateoni.—A register of occupancy by which the holdings of individuals are collected together.

Khudkasht.—See Asāmī and Kāshtkār.

Kūrktehsīl.—The process of temporary attachment, used as a coercive measure.

M

Māfī.—An assignment of the Government revenue of some land, the holder of which was styled māfīdār.

Mahal.—An estate. Arrangements by estates are said to be made mahalwār.

Mahāsil.—The Government revenue actually realised, in contradistinction to the amount assessed.

Malguzārī.—The Government revenue; the owner or village representative who contracts to pay it is known as the Sadr Malgūzār.

Mālikānā.—The share of the gross produce allowed to ousted proprietors as compensation for loss of management.

Mālzāmin.—A surety for the payment of revenue or rent.

Marwat.—A pension in land or money to the heirs of a retainer killed in the owner's service; the holder is known as marwatdār.

Maurūsī.—Hereditary.

Mauza.—A village. When arrangements are made by villages, they are said to be mauzawār.

Mukaddim.—The principal cultivator who often leased the village in the absence of the owner. They were judicially found to be without transferable or heritable rights in Oudh.

Mukurriridar.—See Istimrārdār.

Mustājir.—A farmer, his tenure is called mustājiri; see also Ijāra.

N

Nānkār.—The portion of the gross rental left to the proprietor, in land or money, by the native Government.

Nāzim.—The chief revenue Official of a district under native rule.

P

Pā'ekāsht.—A non-resident cultivator. One who lives in one village and tills in another.

Pakkā.—One who held the lease of a village by virtue of proprietary right was said to hold pakkā. A masonry well is styled a pakkā one.

Pargana.—A sub-division of a district.

Parmsāna.—The quit-rent paid by the class of mortgagees called biswīdārs.

Patwārī.—The village accountant who records all rent arrangements between landlord and tenant, and furnishes the annual accounts.

Pūkhta.—Holding the sub-settlement of a village is so styled; see also Pakkā.

Pūrwa.—A hamlet.

R

Raīyat.—A tenant; see Asāmī, Kāshtkār, &c. The term is applied to all subjects, especially agriculturists, in old Mahomedan works.

Rāja.—A large landowner; a title of honour.

S

Sāir.—Manorial dues from forest, lake, &c.

Shankalap.—A subordinate tenure which locally differs little, if at all, from Birt, which see.

Shūdkār.—An estimate of the probable yield, on inspection, of a standing crop, on which native assessments used generally to be made.

Sīr.—The home farm of the proprietor or sub-proprietor. The land occupied by ex-proprietors is often so called.

Sūba.—A province, the governor of which was known as Sūbadār.

T

Tahsīl.—The next largest territorial sub-division to a district.

Talluka.—A large estate, portions of which are the sole property of the owner, or tallukdār, while the profits of other portions are in whole or in part intercepted by under-proprietors.

Thīkā.—A lease ; see Ijāra and Mustājiri.

W

Wazīr.—The Prime Minister.

Z

Zamīndār.—A landowner, large or small ; from zamīn, land.